An Unillustrious Alliance

**Recent Titles in
Contributions in Afro-American and African Studies**

Education of the African American Adult: An Historical Overview
Harvey G. Neufeldt and Leo McGee, editors

The Wealth of Races: The Present Value of Benefits from Past Injustices
Richard F. America, editor

Black Music in the Harlem Renaissance: A Collection of Essays
Samuel A. Floyd, Jr., editor

Telling Tales: The Pedagogy and Promise of African American Literature for Youth
Dianne Johnson

Ethiopia: Failure of Land Reform and Agricultural Crisis
Kidane Mengisteab

Anancy in the Great House: Ways of Reading West Indian Fiction
Joyce Jonas

The Poet's Africa: Africanness in the Poetry of Nicolás Guillén and Aimé Césaire
Josaphat B. Kubayanda

Tradition and Modernity in the African Short Story: An Introduction to a Literature in Search of Critics
F. Odun Balogun

Politics in the African-American Novel: James Weldon Johnson, W. E. B. Du Bois, Richard Wright, and Ralph Ellison
Richard Kostelanetz

Disfigured Images: The Historical Assault on Afro-American Women
Patricia Morton

Black Journalists in Paradox: Historical Perspectives and Current Dilemmas
Clint C. Wilson II

Dream and Reality: The Modern Black Struggle for Freedom and Equality
Jeannine Swift, editor

An
Unillustrious
Alliance :

THE AFRICAN AMERICAN
AND JEWISH AMERICAN
COMMUNITIES

WILLIAM M. PHILLIPS, JR.

Contributions in Afro-American and African Studies, Number 146

Greenwood Press
New York • Westport, Connecticut • London

Library of Congress Cataloging-in-Publication Data

Phillips, William M.
   An unillustrious alliance : the African American and Jewish
American communities / William M. Phillips, Jr.
      p.   cm. — (Contributions in Afro-American and African
studies, ISSN 0069-9624 ; no. 146)
   Includes bibliographical references and index.
   ISBN 0-313-27776-1 (alk. paper)
   1. Afro-Americans—Relations with Jews. 2. United States—Race
relations. 3. United States—Ethnic relations. I. Title.
II. Series.
   E185.61.P54   1991
305.8'00973—dc20   91-17126

British Library Cataloguing in Publication Data is available.

Library of Congress Catalog Card Number: 91-17126
ISBN: 0-313-27776-1
ISSN: 0069-9624

First published in 1991

Greenwood Press, 88 Post Road West, Westport, CT 06881
An imprint of Greenwood Publishing Group, Inc.

Printed in the United States of America

The paper used in this book complies with the
Permanent Paper Standard issued by the National
Information Standards Organization (Z39.48–1984).

10   9   8   7   6   5   4   3   2   1

I urge my grandmother

Serena Keyes Williamson

and my parents

Eudora Esther Williamson and William McKinley Phillips

to accept this gift in memory of all our conversations

Contents

Introduction

This book is about the relations between two groups — the African American and Jewish American minority communities — in the United States. My goals are to learn what are, and what have been, the features of the relations of these minority communities within American society, to offer a reasonable explanation of that which is found, and to speculate how such findings may be useful in contributing to the resolution of the problems of intergroup conflict and of concerted intergroup actions in racial contexts.

Considerable attention has been given in the social sciences, the humanities, and the mass media to the bonds connecting African and Jewish Americans. A clear record is established of a distinct affinity between these two communities in the United States since the beginning of the twentieth century and plausibly extending back even into the earlier decades of the nineteenth century. It is curious, nevertheless, to note a certain reticence and awkwardness by scholars in treating this affinity between the African American and Jewish American communities[1] and, as well, the apparent failure to incorporate what is known about it directly into that quest for pluralism and equality in American society.

Examination of how the African American and Jewish American communities interact and interacted, and precisely under what situations or conditions, deserves attention in its own right. It is enough now to note that in the usual study of race and ethnic relations within pluralistic American society less attention is paid to the study of relations between minority groups than to the study of relations between the dominant majority of largely European origin and one or the other, largely non-European, subordinate minorities. My primary concern is with the former perspective. In other words, this inquiry is about the character of the behaviors between two minority communities that occupy different positions in the hierarchy of status positions into which the nation's minority groups are customarily ordered. From the perspectives of mainstream social science the African American community usually is found near the bottom of the social status hierarchy; and the Jewish American community routinely is found near the middle of that same hierarchical order.[2]

It is essential to state that the idea of minority group, which includes the notion of minority community, is central to the analytic strategy of this book. In the context of the particularity of the American race relations experience it is reasonable to consider group consciousness as the core of any conception of the term. Regardless of size, location in space, and constituency, in this book a minority group is held to be a social aggregate whose solidarity is both a response to external pressure forcing it to live in some degree of isolation, conflict, and ostracism and a response to internal pressures forcing it to create a distinctive collective consciousness. The African American and Jewish American communities, therefore, are identified as minority groups.[3]

Heretofore, in the usual social science conception of the term minority group, the main concern has been with the nature of relations between minority groups and a dominant, or majority, group. Considerable attention therefore has been directed toward the development of types of minority groups and the conditions of their existence. Ogbu, for instance, presents a minority group typology divided into autonomous, caste (pariah), and immigrant types.[4] Under his formulation African Americans are identified as a caste or pariah minority group and Jewish Americans are seen as an autonomous minority group. It is to be noted, however, that the chief emphasis of this book is with the nature of the relations between minority groups and not with the traditional social science emphasis on the relationships between minority and majority, or dominant, groups.

There is no definite answer to the question of why I chose to approach race and ethnic relations by way of an examination of the relationship between the African American and Jewish American communities. It may be fair to say now that I am haunted by the phenomenon of racism — its origins, manifestations, contributing conditions, metamorphoses, and consequences. I am an African American, born and reared during the decades of the 1920s and 1930s in the southwestern states of Texas and Oklahoma. In the bosom of my family I learned early, for instance, that Japhet Troy Williamson — my mother's father and a school teacher and dry goods store owner — left Texas on June 3, 1893, via Guthrie (Oklahoma), Chicago, New York City, and London (England) to reconnoiter the West Coast of Africa. As children we were led to understand that his action was a response of defiance — a gesture signifying indomitable opposition and intractability, an expression of personal honor and integrity — to the racial tyranny of his time. He returned to Texas in October 1893, fatally ill but bringing ideas, journal notes, and gifts.

In the smaller cities of those southwestern states, and in that time, I experienced behaviors and actions permeated with racial intolerance, prejudice, and discrimination. Such experiences led to an awareness of the existence of Jewish Americans, the common perceptions of them as a pariah group in that region, and the selective propensities of bigotry. Subjection to that cruelty of fate of volunteering for military service out of idealistic zeal for allegedly universal values, and experiencing directly and brutally their apparent negation, contributed to my interest in and pro- vided the opportunity for involvement with the higher learning. At Fisk University and the University of Chicago I was exposed to an approach to the study of society that emphasized conspicuously the issues of race and ethnicity, the work of investigation in knowing, and a commitment to social action. Each and all of these experiences have contributed to my curiosity about the realities of power, conflict, oppression, and liberation as played out in the dramas of intergroup relations.

Within the heterogeneous racial and ethnic pluralism of the United States are several combinations of minority groups from which to choose an area of study. Indeed, perhaps a scholarly need exists to study all of these possible combinations. In my opinion, however, relations of the African American community to the several Hispanic (Chicano, Cuban, Puerto Rican, and others), Asian (Asian Indian, Chinese, Filipino, Japanese, Korean, Pacific Ocean Islander, Vietnamese, and others), and the diverse Native American communities are unlike those of the extended ones between the African American and the Jewish American com- munities. Berson observes, for example, that "the common denominator in the otherwise divergent and even antipathetical histories of the Negroes and the Jews is [a] tradition of separateness; in their inability to merge with the mass that surrounds them, they are alike. Both have been victims of caste systems which viewed them as pariahs, and in this they are unique among Americans."[5]

The above conclusion is to be followed closely in that which follows. Suffice it to say here that the argument to be made is not that the African American and Jewish American communities have been and are unified with respect to their perceptions of and expectations for each other. Rather, the contrary is more likely. That is, the persistent diversities and even contradictions within these two particular communities contribute sharply to the evolving character of their persistent affinity for each other within American society. I shall argue, essentially, that these two American minority communities have experienced histories of prejudice and discrimination — or bigotry, exclusion, and rejection — out of which, as social collectivities of fate and destiny, their unique identities and solidarities have been forged.

The African American and Jewish American communities represent minority groups *par excellence*[6] and as such merit study both for themselves and for the possible application of what is learned to the understanding of minority group relations among all nations or peoples of the world. I believe that within American society — characterized in historical actuality by a distinct ideology and culture blending idiosyncratically individualism, racism, elitism, free trade, international capitalism, and a distinct militarism tilted especially toward an international commitment to the world hegemony of Western European civilization — these two minority communities enact distinctive role performances and have constructed a unique interrelationship within the ever-changing scheme of American race and ethnic relations.

To my knowledge no written records of the coalition formation process or the alliance of the African and Jewish American communities were kept and preserved. There is no one collection of documents available for examining its origins, evolutionary development, and consequences. As a result I had to deduce the reality of the alliance from a large combination of published sources, newspaper articles, and government documents.

The historical limitation or boundaries of this work are left deliberately broad. Indeed, the expectancy for the book is that it address not so much the past as the future in American society. The directions that developments in minority group relations may follow in the United States are its ultimate concern. In looking at the evolving patterns of relations over time between the African American and Jewish American communities — presumed to be exemplars of minority groups linked interactively — I will be trying always to see the play of the group or the collectivity. The emphasis upon the group in trying to understand, and possibly to explain, patterns of relations between racial and ethnic minorities in the United States is followed deliberately despite the general belief or legitimation in American culture of the ideology of individualism. This orientation, in that which follows, cannot be overemphasized; and its importance to the integrity of the examination is to counterbalance the usual tendency to ignore or deny the importance of the reality of groupism in American race relations.[7]

NOTES

1. For a treatment of one explanation of this sensed reserve, see Paul Findley, *They Dare to Speak Out: People and Institutions Confront Israel's Lobby* (Westport, CT: Lawrence Hill & Company, 1985). Also, Edward W. Said touches obliquely on "the immunity from sustained criticism" enjoyed by the Jewish American community and Israel as one of the issues in the article "An Ideology of Difference," to be found in *"Race," Writing and Difference*, edited by Henry Louis Gates, Jr. (Chicago: University of Chicago Press, 1986), p. 38.

2. Comparison of the relative status of minority groups in the American social status hierarchy is complex and, moreover, is a research area that seems to have been approached with much reserve and timidity. Repeated social distance measurement of racial and ethnic groups, which may be interpreted as indices of relative social status, consistently shows that the African American group is assigned positions at the lower end (26, 27, and 29 out of a possible rank of 30) while the Jewish American group consistently is assigned positions in the middle ranks (19, 16, and 15 out of a possible rank of 30) of the social distance scale. See Emory S. Bogardus, "Comparing Racial Distance in Ethiopia, South, and the United States," in *Sociology and Social Research* 52 (1968): 152. Also, according to Lieberson, "the latent structure of whites' racial attitudes is relatively similar regardless of location. North and South, whites are more similar than dissimilar. Furthermore, in a hierarchy of preferences built into this latent structure, blacks are always the last preferred racial/ethnic group." See Stanley Lieberson, *A Piece of the Pie: Blacks and White Immigrants since 1880* (Berkeley: University of California Press, 1981), p. 594.

3. See George E. Simpson and J. Milton Yinger, *Racial and Cultural Minorities* (New York: Harper & Brothers, 1953), pp. 22, 222; Louis Wirth, "The Problems of Minority Groups," in Ralph Linton (ed.), *The Science of Man in the World Crisis* (New York: Columbia University Press, 1945), p. 347; and Robin M. Williams, Jr., *Mutual Accommodation* (Minneapolis: University of Minnesota Press, 1977), p. 53.

4. John U. Ogbu, *Minority Education and Caste* (New York: Academic Press, 1978), pp. 21–25.

5. Lenora E. Berson, *The Negroes and the Jews* (New York: Random House, 1971), p. 13.

6. Here, again, "the Negroes and the Jews have created a web of social, political and economic connections which is at times complementary and at times conflicting, and always complex. Separately, and in combination, these two disparate peoples have played major roles in the social revolution that has transformed twentieth-century America. As allies they are at the core of the liberal movement in the United States" (Berson, *The Negroes and the Jews*, 1971), p. 9.

7. Cruse observes, for instance, about the study of racial and cultural relations in America that "the group question has been misinterpreted and mishandled for many decades." See Harold Cruse, *The Crisis of the Negro Intellectual* (New York: William Morrow & Co., 1967), pp. 483–484.

Acknowledgments

Encouragement and sound advice for this book came from a host of former students, friends, and family members. Parts of the manuscript were read and suggestions offered by Professors Hylan Lewis and Rhoda Lois Blumberg. My brother-in-law, Professor Sherman Beverly, Jr., of Northeastern Illinois University, and my brother, Waldo Bruce Phillips, disagreed with some aspects of my arguments but enthusiastically supported my courage in attempting such a vast subject. My cousin, Professor Audrey Lawson Vinson of Alabama A. & M. University, graciously assumed copy-editing responsibilities and thereby, with her writing skills, careful eye, and infinite patience, reduced the gap between my thoughts and their expression. Attorney Lennox S. Hinds exemplified for me the epitome of generosity and collegiality and Ms. Ruth Ercell Vaughn, a classmate, indeed did keep the faith. For technical computer assistance I am grateful to Janet Salowe and William H. Greenhalgh of the Rutgers University Center for Computer and Information Services. A first draft of this book was begun during a 1986–87 faculty leave from Rutgers, The State University of New Jersey. My thanks also go to the University Research Council for financial assistance through grant 2-02171. Lastly, I must thank Marie Y. Beverly for being my wife.

An
Unillustrious
Alliance

1

The Issues and Approach

One of the most profound puzzles of American democracy historically has been that of racial inequality. This matter, initially, was of grave concern to the designers of the National Constitution (the great compromise of the Constitution, allegedly, was slavery). It continued to attract attention in those studies of the commingling of the messianic and civil republican traditions in America by James Bryce in *The American Commonwealth*[1] and Alexis de Tocqueville in *Democracy in America*.[2] It permeates the phenomena of the 1984 and 1988 presidential election campaigns, centering especially on the candidacy of Jesse Jackson. This puzzle of racial inequality reverberated in the furor following the remarks about African Americans in September 1986 by Prime Minister Yasuhiro Nakasone of Japan. It haunts the myriad struggles in the United States, and throughout the world, against the apartheid system of the Republic of South Africa. The purpose of this book, ultimately, is to understand the intransigence of this puzzle of racial inequality in a modern democracy and to contribute to resolving it.

The enormity of this general task should be clear to all, as the attempts to perform it are legend. That particular aspect of the general task to be examined here is the processes of interrelations — negotiating, bargaining, cooperating, and conflicting — that have bound together almost inextricably the African American and Jewish American communities. Such an examination includes, too, paying some attention to selected contextual features of American society — for example, historical, political, economic, and ideological changes — which can be presumed reasonably to underlie the interrelationships mentioned above. The essential issues are, then, to identify and describe those interrelations existing largely in the twentieth century between these two minority communities within pluralistic American society and to learn the possible meanings of these relations as they bear upon the promise and problems of racial inequality.

A cursory look must be taken at prominent or conspicuous features of that abstraction commonly called the social and cultural system of American society. This is obligatory because the historical interplay of the African and Jewish American communities is performed always within the boundaries of that abstraction — American society — taken to represent the changing and complex realities of the American variant of Western civilization. In this chapter, also, the themes and analytical ideas to be used throughout this examination of the relations between these two minority communities will be presented.

THE AMERICAN REPUBLIC

The essential national character of the American people is the pivot from which one can attempt to identify and describe patterned relations — negotiating, bargaining, cooperating, and conflicting — between the African American and Jewish American communities. Civic republicanism, in part a response to the corruption and oppression of the Old World (essentially Western European civilization), a unique value system, and an incessant jostling of social change can serve here as key clues toward some appreciation of the essence of the national American character.

The notion of arrangements to minimize risks for some societal groups, and to constrain tensions between the racial, class, and ethnic elements of the pluralistic system — that singular structure of social heterogeneity so distinctive of American society — comes early to mind in considering the pristine origins and the practices of republican self-government in the United States. Constitutional government is the basic risk-controlling arrangement, and it becomes meaningful pragmatically out of the operation of at least four principles. These are the people as constituent power; the separation of powers (with its checks and balances as the way of having a pluralistic, policy-making, sharing-of-power system within the basic separation structure); federalism (the division of sovereignty); and the idea that the Constitution, as text and document, is authoritative and must be consulted. This American structure of constitutional government is, and always is, becoming. It is constantly kept lively through contests of public interest and public purpose, conservatism and reform, and promised ideal and failure of practice in the matter of equalitarianism. This governmental system is essentially a contest between the virtues and defects of liberalism and the sanctified destiny and redemptive mission of a messianic tradition.[3]

The control of tensions — potential, emergent, and actual — between those status groups (primarily of class, racial, and ethnic derivation) making up the pluralistic structure of American society through a transactional process for collective survival or self-interest is also seen as distinctive. Regardless of the myth of individualism in American ideology, it will be assumed in this book that status groups are the fundamental units of society and that the fundamental struggle for scarce resources — symbolic or material — occurs between such groups.

The consequences of this assumed position are presumed to be important for understanding the relational interplay between the African American and the Jewish American communities in modern America. Thus, the scarce resources contested for by status groups may be economic, political, social, and symbolic. From such contests emerge, among other things, behavior or action structures of hierarchy: privilege, license or liberty versus disadvantage; dominance versus dependency and subordination; prestige versus stigma; and power versus submission or powerlessness. And, out of the flux of behavior from which these hierarchical structures emerge, there is a tendency toward organization of the groups into what appears to be a harmonious, balanced, more or less stable, ranked order of social status that is held here to be a distinctive element of the essential national character of America.

A set of what may be called basic Western values, or a variant thereof called the Eurocentric philosophy,[4] is the core of the American value system. Derived largely from a kind of melding of Greco-Roman and Judeo-Christian judgments about the nature of man and the nature of society — and providing the foundation for the dynamics of a capitalist economy and the system of republican self-government described above — traditional American values have evolved as representative cultural responses about the acquisition, maintenance, and utilization of social power for particular environmental and societal conditions. These basic, and what are often considered by many philosophers of science to be universally valid, values are: the belief in human reason, the uniqueness of each individual (who possesses rights), the voluntary nature of obligations to the community, the rule of law, the value of work, and a sense of consciousness of kind or virulent ethnocentrism involving a conviction about collective racial superiority, the most benign measure of which is benevolent paternalism toward non-Anglo-Saxon races.

That decided societal tendency toward the acceptance of adaptive change must be added to civic republicanism, racial and ethnic pluralism, and a core set of values as clues for reaching some understanding of the national American character. Social change is used here to mean the process, and its consequences, of continuous alternation and balance between unlike or opposing social interaction. More formally, social change has been seen as that transition from one relatively stable structural-cultural-characterological system toward another.[5] Serious attention has been given by those who study American society (and by those studying racial and ethnic relations) to this feature in our national character of quick acceptance of adaptive change at least since the formulation by Ogburn of the hypothesis of cultural lag.[6]

But in the deeper realities of the apparent rigidity of that structured order of status inequality of minority groups in America, appearances of change are not to be trusted. Does the "right" question to be asked about change in race relations concern itself with eventual change (that is, progress) or with the actual gap — allowing the inference of an apparent lack of significant change — in status inequality between minority groups now or at some particular point in time? It is not argued that the persistence of status inequality or expected change, that is, progress, is the more basic societal reality although it is conceded that the acceptance of either assumption could have different analytic consequences. The position I take is that social change is normal and that, as reality, it assumes distinct prominence in any effort to appreciate essential and distinguishing elements of any culture, but more particularly, social change in American society.[7]

Evidence in support of the idea of adaptive change being a distinguishing feature of the national American character is abundant from the decade of the 1890s with the appearance of the doctrine of "separate but equal" and the 1898 adventure of the Spanish-American War, to the national administration in the 1980s of Ronald Reagan. Cycling incessantly throughout these nine decades, and having immense implications for the status inequality of minority groups in America, were massive societal and cultural processes and forces demanding adaptation. Some examples of these forces and the apparent adaptations follow.

During what has been called by some scholars of race and ethnic relations the Age of Booker T. Washington, the embedding of the infamous "jim crow" system into the regional way of life of the South was essentially completed. At the same time, the gentlemen's agreement of 1908 involving the exclusion of Asian (largely Japanese) immigration was being put into force. The appearance and persistence of purposeful hatred of Jews and their superb efforts toward survival, accommodation, and assimilation following the great Jewish immigration movements between 1881–1914 and 1935–1955 indicate adaptability of the social status system of America.

Adaptability is shown also in the pre–World War I population movement as well as that massive relocation (The Great Migration), beginning about 1915, of African Americans from the agrarian rural and semirural to the industrial urban and metropolitan way of life. The passage of the National Recovery Act of 1932 and the subsequent emergence of unionism (especially with the founding of the Congress of Industrial Organizations [CIO] in 1935), as well as passage of the 1954 Supreme Court decision about racially segregated schools and the Civil Rights Act of 1965 are crucial examples of legislative and judicial reform coinciding with the transformation from passive to active participation of heretofore oppressed minority communities in societal change.

The technological base driving American society has undergone, during the decades of our concern, what may be called a metamorphosis. Transformations in the realms of energy use, means of communication and transportation, machine and tool technic, and the so-called high-tech revolution culminate now in the goal of technological development essential for the successful exploration of outer space, which is seen as the new frontier. Associated with such deep and, in some instances, rapid changes are new ideas and knowledge bases about the nature of time, manpower utilization, designed organizations for managing the partnerships of humans and natural resources required and, eventually, the conservation of the physical environment. While it is not argued that the interrelations of the African American and Jewish American communities are to be explained by such technological change, it is reasonable to expect that the collective perceptions and responses of these minority communities to such environmental conditions would contribute to the shaping of their alliance or coalition relations.

Between the 1890s and now there is difficulty in conceiving analytically of any domain of American life in which adaptive change did occur that was insignificant for understanding minority group interrelations. Radical innovation took place throughout the popular or mass culture in the ways in which members of minority groups were perceived. Note, for example, the crystallization in popular music and entertainment of the "crossover" phenomenon as illustrated by the careers of Michael Jackson, Pearl Bailey, and Bill Cosby. Attention is called to the strategic uses made of the mass media, especially television, to influence opinion and possibly modify behavior affecting the status of minority groups in American society. For example, note the media coverage, especially throughout the South, of civil rights activities and, throughout the nation, of the Black Nationalist movements.

Within the media of mass communication, and the fine, performing, and the more spontaneous arts those customarily invidious norms governing the roles of African Americans, for example, appear to have been drastically altered. A glance at the variety of forms of mass behavior exhibited by social movements between 1900 and the present demonstrate the uses made by both the African and Jewish American communities of collective means for engaging in actions specifically designed to induce change in the prevailing legitimate order of status inequality. Associated with much of this adaptability in the realms of technology, idea sets, knowledge bases, and mass culture, simultaneously, was the destruction of some of the customarily held myths, taboos, and images concerning minority groups and their members.

The above brief overview of the undoubted intertwining of massive adaptive change in American society with the hierarchical social status order of minority groups, and the potential consequences for change in the value sphere, do not permit ignoring that the United States, during the nine decades looked at here, was bound inescapably in networks of changing relationships with other nations and groups of nations throughout the world. These networks of changing relationships are illustrated by such examples as the formation and maintenance of the North Atlantic Treaty Organization (NATO) and the South East Asia Treaty Organization (SEATO). For now, attention merely is called to a postulated link between domestic or internal change with international change that is important for understanding alterations in minority community relations in America.

Thus, the change in the fate and destiny of the British Empire, especially during the twentieth century, would appear to have been at work in altering our national interests in and connections with worldwide imperialism and colonialism. Again, the long political and cultural tradition of the Zionist movement culminating by 1917 in the Balfour Declaration — in which the British government announced to the world that it viewed with favor a Jewish national home in Palestine — and the subsequent creation in 1947–1948 of the state of Israel would appear to have had fateful implications for the Jewish American community. These developments will be seen to have crucial significance for the relational process between the African American and the Jewish American communities. In these cited instances of nation-building and international survival, and others that can be recalled, the United States has had an increasingly central role, especially since World War II, and domestic and foreign policies of the nation reveal this clearly. One stark example is the scandal of the American presidency revealed in the 1987 congressional hearings on the sale of military materials to Iran.

The struggles for independence of African nations, and the emergence of that coalition of nations described usually as the Third World or the periphery, strikingly reveal the interlocking of American foreign and domestic policies with profound implications for the quest for status equality by American minority communities. Those classical aims of American foreign policy since at least World War II — the containment of the Soviet Union and pursuing an economic and geopolitical strategy whose cumulative consequences are the preservation and legitimation of a hegemony of dominance over the so-called developing nations of the world — illustrate how difficult it is to separate the confounding effects of domestic and international policies from the changing relations of minority communities within the nation. While perhaps tenuous, the suggested linkage between the foreign policy aims of the United States and the liberation and survival objectives of African nations and the so-called Third World and other developing nations seems reasonable. Contradictions between such linkages historically have been, and are, used by racial and ethnic communities in America to further their particular interests in domestic policy formation. Moreover, the incessant efforts within the political process of the United States to resolve such contradictions (for example, the Solidarity movement of Poland and the Polish American community) would appear to be strong evidence of the interlocking of American foreign and domestic policies with almost certain implications for the dynamics of minority community relationships.

Providing the broad boundaries of the national character of the American people was the objective of this section.[8] This background had to be looked at, deliberately, before trying to see the complex interrelationships of the African and Jewish American communities. Without such an elaborate or detailed explication, but accepting the proposition that status groups are the basic analytic unit of society and that purposive, interactive behavior for limited resources occurs most importantly between groups, sketches were made of four essential elements of the national character of America. These are our civic republicanism or constitutional government; our unique status-ordered arrangement of racial and ethnic pluralism; the predominately Eurocentric value system; and our pronounced receptivity to adaptive social and cultural change.

In looking at this general background the following observations reasonably can be made about the historical situation of the Jewish American community. And, it must be noted, it is impossible to imagine such observations being made about the historical situation of the African American community.

> The history of the Jews in the United States has been — so far — a history of good times, of expectations realized. There were times of trial and trouble, but even at their worse they never compared in scope or in malignancy to the calamities that befell the European Jew. In the United States, Jews prospered as never before in their history. The United States was the first country in the world to give the Jews political equality and religious liberty, enabling them, as no other nation-state had, fully to exercise their rights as citizens and, at the same time, freely to observe their religion, sustain their traditions, and perpetuate their culture.[9]

PERSPECTIVE AND APPROACH

The evidence is overwhelming that in the United States, at least from approximately 1890 to the present, there is a legacy of a singular set of perceptions, definitions, expectations, and experiences between those making up the African and Jewish American communities.[10] It is assumed that within this legacy lies that sad wisdom of minority groups universally — the knowledge of how to survive. Accepting the reality of this legacy permits the inference of a voluntary, mutual commitment of the African and Jewish American communities to engage in interactive behavior leading to concerted actions for the satisfaction, at least, of common goals.

A perspective or orientation and several sets of concepts are employed as an approach to examine the process of becoming, continuity, and limits making up this legacy of behavior evolving over nine decades between the African American and Jewish American communities. First, this examination is guided by the notion that a collective or group, rather than an individualistic, orientation is required to obtain the surest knowledge about the ordered, relational behaviors between these two minority communities. Acceptance of this notion of the superiority of a collective or group approach derives in large part, in my judgment, from the distressing overemphasis in the scholarly and popular literatures on the play of psychological, individualistic, and leadership factors in understanding the dynamics of race and ethnic relations.

Thus, above all else, it will be argued that the experiences of African Americans and Jewish Americans ultimately must be explained as the actions of collectivities called minority communities and that minority communities, as social entities, are to be perceived abstractly as subsets of status groups operating within the almost chaotic and unpredictable phenomenon called American society. As stated earlier, then, a minority community (for example, the African American or the Jewish American collectivity, regardless of size, location in space, or constituency) is held to be a social aggregate whose solidarity or unity is both a response to external pressures forcing it to live in terms of some degree of isolation, conflict, and ostracism and internal pressures forcing it to create a distinctive collective or group consciousness.[11]

Second, the idea of alliance or coalition formation is assumed to be central to any examination of the myriad relationships of survival created in the United States by the African American and Jewish American communities.[12] The process of alliance or coalition formation involves minimally two levels. On the first level there are the notions of the recognition of mutual interests, the will to concerted actions, and an assumption of compatible or joint sharing of powers of regulation or governance between the two minority communities. On the second level, the interaction or relational behaviors between the allies or partners in the alliance takes the form of the core social processes of negotiating, bargaining, cooperating, and conflicting. These processes of interaction, in other words, constitute the essence of the alliance or coalition process between the African American and Jewish American communities. Thus, the behavioral outcomes of these four processes are presumed to be concerted actions — strategic and tactical — by these two minority communities for the attainment of joint purposes or goals within limits imposed by the changing situational context of American society.

To help in interpreting the evidence, derived largely from searches of the scholarly and popular literatures, of interactions between and of collective actions by the African American and Jewish American communities the two constructs of domination (control) and power are applied. Hegemony — which is viewed in the political economy sense of a hierarchy of group privilege, domination, and control within the cauldron of racial and ethnic relations in American society — is not a despised position from which to attempt to understand a particular set of intergroup behavior. Neither is the concept of perceived or actual social power — the capacity of a collective entity (a social group) openly or clandestinely to decide and to have its way despite the resistance of others — unimportant for understanding strategic and tactical actions involving legitimation and authority in inducing change or insuring the continuity of a culturally ingrained order of race relations.

A four-step procedure is used to tease meaning out of both the evidence about interactive behavior between the two minority communities and their collective actions. First, the determination is made that, illustratively, interactive behavior did exist or take place. There has to be, in other words, a clear record of negotiating, bargaining, cooperating, or conflicting. Second, an assessment is made of the conditions, reasons for, and expected goals of such behavior. Third, the attempt is made to discover what appears to be the decisions or agreed-upon policy resulting from the interactive behavior. At this stage of the procedure attention is directed both to anticipated or expected ends as well as to preferred, optional, and proscribed means. And, finally, a conclusion is reached about the results or consequences of implementing the concerted efforts agreed upon for the character of the alliance or coalition.

Essential for the success of the above approach is clarity about the key concept of community. It is described simply by Louis Wirth in terms of "its ability to act corporately. It has a common set of attitudes and values based upon common traditions, similar experiences, and common problems. In spite of its geographical separateness it is welded into a community because of conflict and pressure from without and collective action within."[13] A central element of the orientation of this book is the perception of the African and Jewish American minority groups as communities in the above sense. The Jewish American community is limited by an estimated 1980 population of 5,921,205, or less than 3 percent of the total U.S. population (the 1988 U.S. Jewish population is estimated to be 5,935,000).[14] And, similarly, the African American community is limited by an estimated 1980 population of 26,495,025, or approximately 11.7 percent of the total U.S. population; the 1990 African-American population of the United States is estimated to be between 31,364,000 and 31,959,000.[15]

In giving meaning to the available evidence, and guided by the above orientations and procedures, selected key events in American society judged to be significant for the dynamics of race relations are identified and examined for particular time periods between approximately 1890 and 1990. Those events considered most appropriate for examination generally are restricted to local and national activities in contested arenas such as racial discrimination, segregation, and conflict, the activities of civil rights organizations and movements, and issues involving local, state, and federal governments and national political parties.

Mention must be made here of the scattered locations throughout the United States (for example, urban places and metropolitan areas, the southern region, and the North) of selected events to be used illustratively in examining the reality of an alliance or a coalition. The role of place in determining general and particular characteristics or phases of the alliance between these two minority communities cannot be denied, and this issue deserves analysis on its own merits.

Nevertheless, attention is called to the possibility of place influencing somewhat the process of alliance and coalition (for example, the lynching of Leo M. Frank in Marietta, Georgia; the saga of the Scottsboro Boys and the infamous Tuskegee syphilis experiment in Alabama; the killing fields [lynching and mob violence] of the deep South; recurrent civil disturbances and riots in New York City, Chicago, Detroit, Los Angeles, Newark, and other urban places; the intrigues of the Communist and Socialist Parties with the African American community, especially in New York City, Chicago, and Philadelphia; the traumas of school desegregation throughout the school districts of the nation; the mobilization process [especially organizationally] of the African American community for mainstream political participation by way of civil rights organizing, to city councils, to the office of mayor, and to presidential candidacy throughout the nation; and the epic struggle over school control enacted in New York City). The presumption to be held throughout this book — regardless of place — is that the alliance or coalition between the African American and Jewish American communities permeates or blankets all of the United States.

Any serious attempt to understand particular aspects of the complex saga of racial and ethnic relations in American society must include some recognition of the role of the State. Consideration of federal intervention (executive, legislative, and judicial) in the domain of race relations contributes implicitly to the rather arbitrary organization of the period from 1890 to the present into six segments. These time segments are: The Nadir of Injustice and Inequality (1890–1919); Between World Wars (1920–1939); Dilemmas of War and Peace (1940–1953); Schooling and Equal Rights (1954–1965); The Black Power Movement (1966–1979); and The 1980s.

This largely inductive approach[16] for examining the relational behaviors of the African American and Jewish American communities will be driven by two imperatives: that of dispassionate and rational treatment of evidence about the behavior of people organized racially into groups and that of the application of the results of such an examination to transforming and clarifying the understanding of some basic issues of freedom and justice in a democratic society.

NOTES

1. Selections from *The American Commonwealth*. Social Science 2, The College (Chicago: The University of Chicago Bookstore, 1946).

2. Alexis de Tocqueville, *Democracy in America* (New York: Alfred A. Knopf, Inc., 1945).

3. Arthur M. Schlesinger, Jr., *The Cycles of American History* (Boston: Houghton Mifflin Company, 1985).

4. See Molefi Kete Asante, "Intercultural Communication," in *Working Papers: International Conference on Black Communication,* edited by Bruce E. Williams and Orlando L. Taylor (Bellagio, Italy: The Rockefeller Foundation, 1980), pp. 1–18.

5. J. Milton Yinger, "Presidential Address: Countercultures and Social Change," *American Sociological Review* 42:6 (December 1977): 849.

6. William Fielding Ogburn, *Social Change* (New York: The Viking Press, 1950), pp. 200–13. Ogburn's view "is that the several parts of modern culture are not changing at the same rate, some parts are changing much more rapidly than others; and since there is a correlation and interdependence of parts, a rapid change in one part of our culture requires readjustments through other changes in the various correlated parts of culture," pp. 201–2.

7. A statement attributed by John Steinbeck to Marcus Aurelius sharply defines this position. "Observe constantly that all things take place by change, and accustom thyself to consider that the nature of the universe loves nothing so much as to change things which are and to make new things like them. For everything that exists is in a manner the seed of that which will be." John Steinbeck, *East of Eden* (New York: Penguin Books, 1979), p. 647.

8. The perils of this undertaking are not ignored. For a succinct summary of such perils in examining the American national character see Alex Inkeles, "The American Character," *The Center Magazine* 16:6 (November/December 1983): 25–39. Inkeles' emphasis tends largely to be upon societal continuity and may be taken as a fair representation of contemporary mainstream sociological thinking upon this topic. Illustratively, when discussing racial injustice he stresses "a long-term process of social and structural change" in the basic American character toward intolerance rather than the stability and persistence (or continuity) in the social order of America of racial discrimination and injustice. "I believe that tolerance of religious, sexual, and racial differences in the United States has been quite substantially and steadily increasing over the last twenty-five years." Who could quarrel with this statement? But, this choice of emphasis, or raising the question in this way, is to me a curious feature of mainstream sociological inquiry. Followed to its deepest reach, framing the question in this way tends to block the possibility of learning why and how the social order so selectively retains and changes as it does; and it deemphasizes learning about how to resolve the discriminating effects of such alleged societal continuities upon all groups of American citizens. Note, for example, this portion of his conclusion: "I consider the elements of the American character structure that have been most persistent to be those most essential to the continued functioning of a modern democratic policy governing a large-scale, industrial, technological society." This statement would seem to deflect and obscure learning about the continuity of injustice toward and the persistence of status inequality of minority groups.

9. Lucy S. Davidowicz, "A Century of Jewish History, 1881–1981: The View from America," *American Jewish Year Book — 1982* (New York: The Jewish Publication Society of America and The American Jewish Committee, 1981), pp. 97–98.

10. For a critique of this evidence see the Bibliographic Essay.

11. For instance, Blackwell defines the African American community as "a highly diversified set of interrelated structures and aggregates of people who are held together by the forces of white oppression and racism." See James A. Blackwell, *The Black Community: Diversity and Unity* (New York: Harper & Row, 1975), p. xiii. Also see Chapter 10, "The Black Community in a White Society."

12. Gamson defines an alliance or coalition simply as "the joint use of resources by two or more social units." William A. Gamson, "A Theory of Coalition Formation," in *Small Groups: Studies in Social Interaction,* edited by A. Paul Hare, et al. (New York: Alfred A. Knopf, 1965), p. 564.

13. Louis Wirth, *The Ghetto* (Chicago: The University of Chicago Press, 1956), p. 290. The idea of the construct community is vague and elusive. An excellent, and more recent, delineation of it may be found in Philip Selznick, "The Demands of The Community," *The Center Magazine* 20:1 (January/February 1987): 35–36.

14. The American Jewish Committee, *American Jewish Year Book,* Vol. 82 (New York: The Jewish Publication Society of America, 1982), Table 1, p. 168; and The American Jewish Committee, *American Jewish Year Book,* Vol. 89 (New York: The Jewish Publication Society of America, 1989), p. 233.

15. U.S. Bureau of the Census, *U.S. Summary — Characteristics of the Population* (Washington, DC: U.S. Bureau of the Census, 1983), Table 39, pp. 20–22; and U.S. Bureau of the Census, *U.S. Level Preliminary Post-Enumeration Survey (PES) Estimates of Total Population* (Washington, DC: U.S. Bureau of the Census, 1991), Table 3, p. 5.

16. Risk is involved in attempting to get knowledge useful for the development of public policy from research in the area of racial and ethnic relations. Theory dealing with the development of human and civil rights and social policy is muddled. According to Walter Korpi, "Power, Politics, and State Autonomy in the Development of Social Citizenship," *American Sociological Review* 54:3 (June 1989): 311–14, for example, there is considerable uncertainty among theoretical positions about "the extent to which they view social policy development as a result of rational actions of individuals or collectivities, as well as with respect to the relative role in this process assigned to factors such as group and class conflict, the distribution of power resources, political parties, parliamentary processes, interest organizations, and the autonomous actions of state officials." Regardless of this potential handicap, however, one of the goals of this work about relations between minority communities in a pluralistic society is to contribute knowledge useful for public policy determination involving preferential entitlement in such areas as employment, housing, workers' compensation, health, public manufacturing and construction contracts, mortgage assistance, loans, job promotions, the Armed Services, and education.

2

The Nadir of Injustice and Inequality: 1890–1919

The citizenry of the United States during the 1890s and throughout most of the first two decades of the twentieth century was engaged furiously in adapting to and coping with massive social forces. On the international scene these social forces may be identified as, first, the closing out of the nation's most intense period of imperialist expansion and the fulfillment of its mandate of "manifest destiny." Involved here was the acquisition of Puerto Rico, Hawaii, and the Philippines and the establishment of hegemony throughout the Caribbean Islands and in the nations of Central and South America. Second, there was a drastic alteration in the nation's role internationally. This involved a conspicuously increased participation in the entrenchment of Western European hegemony over the rest of the peoples and nations of the world. The nation was embarking upon acceptance of the role of a superpower, which entailed becoming a kind of surrogate for the heretofore colonial powers of Western Europe in their historic control and exploitation of the peoples of Africa, Asia, and the Middle East.

Simultaneously, but on the domestic scene, the citizens of the nation grappled with at least six sets of almost inseparable social forces. These were the closing of the frontier; the transformation from essentially an agrarian to a predominately industrial, technological, and corporate capitalist economy; the manpower, racist, and diplomatic issues of unlimited immigration; the shifting from a largely rural to an essentially urban way of life; the solidification of a stratified structure featuring at its apex a privileged Anglo-Saxon, Protestant, elite which — it has been argued — dominated American society; and legitimation of the processes of exclusion, in theory and in fact, of African Americans from democracy and justice.

The definitive examination of the above societal forces is not our purpose here. But locating and describing instances of alliance or coalition between the African and Jewish American communities during this particular period can be done only within the situational context set by these same societal forces. Thus, in this chapter brief profiles are drawn of the African and Jewish American communities against the background of a situational context bounded by the social forces identified above. How these two minority communities tended to define or give meaning to what can be viewed as a common social context, and the kind of organized responses they seemed to make to it, are the objectives of these brief descriptive profiles. Then, an overview of the interrelations created by the two minority communities during this period will complete the chapter.

THE AFRICAN AMERICAN COMMUNITY

Within seven months of the death of Frederick Douglass in 1895, Booker T. Washington, principal of Tuskegee Institute of Tuskegee, Alabama, delivered his famed speech at the Atlanta, Georgia, Cotton States Exposition. There were two apparent effects of this speech, at least from the viewpoint of the political, governmental, philanthropic, and industrial/corporate elites of the time. It secured for Washington the symbolic title of race leader; and it legitimated the almost complete exclusion of African Americans from the mainstream political, economic, and cultural processes of the nation — one of the primary manifest objectives of that infamous post–Reconstruction Era system of "jim crow." In 1915, Booker T. Washington died. The years between these two dates, and those immediately preceding and following them, are undoubtedly one of the most dismal periods in the history of the nation for the survival of the African American community.

Often called the late post–Reconstruction Era by historians, the African American community during this time experienced, in its attempt to arrive at a collective identity and consciousness, a combination of singularly unique conditions of violence and brutality, degradation, oppression, and exploitation. The Hayes-Tilden agreement of 1877, a bargain ostensibly reached between the national Democratic and Republican Parties and the interests they represented, allowed the presidency to go to Rutherford B. Hayes. The significance of this agreement for our purposes here was the political redefinition at the national level of the societal situation concerning African Americans. Thus, effective social control and power in matters concerning the recently freed slaves was shifted from the federal to the state governments. In this relocation the matter of the fulfillment of the promises of citizenship for African Americans, and their acceptance as equals in America, is relegated from a central decisive national issue to a local, regional, or sectional matter. This decision of political expediency is the bedrock from which emerged, during the decades between 1890-1920, those peculiar and confounding conditions to be defined and resolved by the African American community.[1]

In 1896 the U.S. Supreme Court handed down the *Plessy* v. *Ferguson* decision following its 1893 decision declaring unconstitutional the Civil Rights Act of 1875, which enfranchised and attempted to insure the protection of African Americans freed from slavery.[2] As consequences of these two decisions the doctrine of white supremacy, prima facie, was legitimated constitutionally, and African Americans were subject to the infamous institution of "jim crow." This meant that separation, segregation, and invidious discrimination against them, especially in the southern states, was sanctioned legally. Furthermore, the processes of political disenfranchisement of African Americans was made legal. In other words, participation by African Americans in the democratic process, ideally and actually, was inhibited and severely curtailed.

Attempts by the African American community during the earlier years of this period to develop strategic allies tended generally to be unsuccessful. Trying to be included in the People's Party, or the Populist Movement, ended with African Americans eventually becoming targets of terrorism — including brutality, intimidation, and killings — as well as being dispossessed of property. The inability to resolve the tension between the two doctrines of white supremacy and of working class solidarity prevented genuine involvement of African Americans in the emergence of worker organizations. Especially was this so in the instance of that shift in policy from African American inclusion to their exclusion by the American Federation of Labor.[3] The social reality, therefore, which the African American community had to recognize and confront included, as in the instance of the political process, their systematic restriction if not exclusion from meaningful or equitable participation in both the agrarian and the industrial and technological revolutions through which the nation was passing. Interestingly, however, African Americans during this time were allowed to participate rather actively in imperialistic adventures against Cuba, the Philippine Islands, Hawaii, and Puerto Rico. In these adventures African American sailors of the USS *Maine* and African American enlisted men of the 24th and 25th Infantry and the 9th and 10th Cavalry, U.S. Regular Army, exhibited distinguished heroism in fighting and dying despite what has been described as shabby or racist tactical and strategic deployment.[4] A few years afterwards in what was

known as the Brownsville Incident of 1906 or the "Black Dreyfus Affair"
— the only documented case of mass punishment in the history of the
U.S. Army — 167 men in three companies of the First Battalion, 25th
Infantry, were summarily — that is, without court-martial or trial —
discharged without honor following alleged racial disturbances in Fort
Brown, Texas.[5] Events such as these, with their attendant stigma,
negative imagery, and disillusionment, undoubtedly contributed to the
processes of identity formation and collective solidarity then being
constructed by the African American community.

A most threatening aspect of the reality, in the situational context, of
the period that could not be ignored by the African American community
was its being the object of a regime of terror. The flavor of this regime is
evoked by Foster's summary description:

> One of the worst pogroms occurred in Wilmington, North Carolina, in 1898.
> Nine Negroes massacred outright; and a score wounded and hunted like
> partridges on the mountain. In August, 1900, a mob raged through the streets
> of New York, beating Negroes. In 1906, in Atlanta, Georgia, a riot lasted
> four days, with several Negroes and whites killed. Springfield, Ohio, had two
> "race riots" within a few years, and Greensburg, Indiana, was the scene of
> another at about the same time. But the worst one was in Springfield,
> Illinois, in Lincoln's town, in August, 1908. These were the years, too, of a
> great number of lynchings. Between 1900 and 1914 there were recorded no
> less than 1,079 Negroes brutally murdered by armed mobs. The lynchings
> were usually carried out with the full knowledge and consent, and sometimes
> with the actual participation, of the local authorities.[6]

Little evidence is available about the experiences, during this regime
of terror, of that majority of the African American citizenry who resided
in the rural areas and the small towns and cities of America. There are no
reasons to suspect that they, largely because of residential location and
way of life, escaped the pervasive dehumanization, intimidation, and
humiliation of the terrorism of the time.

One of the most shocking and disillusioning experiences of African
Americans during this period of the war to make the world safe for
democracy was their treatment by official or public agencies as well as by
the behaviors of individuals and organizations in the nonpublic sector.[7]
The shame felt and the shock and disappointment derived from these
experiences must be considered reasonably to have contributed lasting
and profound effects on the collective consciousness of the African
American community. For example, 57 delegates representing the African
diaspora throughout the world — including African Americans in

prominent leadership roles — convened in Paris, France, at the time of the Peace Conference in an attempt to secure international relief from such outrages.[8] Nevertheless, expressions of racial intolerance within America, culminating again in a regime of terror, peaked during the post-war years. According to Quarles:

> In the year following World War I, the United States witnessed a series of race riots unprecedented in numbers and in violence. Of the more than twenty such disturbances that broke out in 1919 in cities from Omaha, Nebraska, to Longview, Texas, the most serious outbreak took place in Chicago. When order was restored [in Chicago], the dead numbered thirty-eight and the wounded totaled 537. The burning and destruction of property left hundreds of families homeless.[9]

The adaptive responses of the African American community to this hostile situational context were diverse. First, there was the emergence and peaking within the African American community of that complex ideological and leadership controversy involving educational and political roles and expectations in the United States. Variously called the Trotter-Dubois versus Booker T. Washington crisis, the industrial versus liberal arts philosophy of education controversy, or the radical versus conservative political solution to racism, this issue served simultaneously to unify and to divide the African American community.[10] It unified by heightening a consciousness of being, individually and collectively, the target or victim of the racist social order. It was divisive by creating links between members of the African American community and elements of the European American majority allowing both possible cooptation of leadership as well as dissent over the legitimacy of, and the continuity of control over, the racist social order.

Second, a definitive voluntary association and special-interest group structure within the African American community began to emerge. A singular feature of this emergent organizational structure was the preeminence of the church — an institution of the sacred domain of American culture. These sacred institutions of the African American community were largely Protestant Christian and tended to be marked by a conspicuous absence of direct European American control. Other elements of this emergent organizational structure include the creation in 1900 of the National Negro Business League and the founding of the Niagara Movement in 1905. Many of the fraternal orders (Prince Hall Masonry, the Eastern Stars, the Odd Fellows, the Elks, Queen Esther Courts, and Knights of Pythias), the mutual aid or benevolent societies, and the social lodges of the African American community — a legacy of the Reconstruction and even earlier eras — flourished during this period. Almost all of the Greek-letter fraternities and sororities of the African American community were founded during this period.

In 1909 the National Association for the Advancement of Colored People (NAACP) emerged, and between 1911 and 1913 the National Urban League began operations. Communication and specialized information needs of this emergent community organizational structure were met by the development of a national media network of newspapers and magazines. These included, for example, *The Baltimore Afro American* beginning in 1892, *The New York Age* in 1895, *The Chicago Defender* in 1905, *The Norfolk Journal and Guide* in 1910, *The Pittsburgh Courier* and *The Crisis* in 1910, and *The Messenger* in 1917.[11]

The appearance during these years of what has been called the middle-class-in-emergence should be included as a significant part of this process of structural reorganization of the African American community. Redding describes the "emerging middle class of decent domestic servants, small tradesmen, part-time lawyers, and night-time doctors who were becoming extremely vocal on such subjects as race discrimination, Negro rights, and Negro solidarity, and who . . . were learning the uses of political power even as they slowly acquired it."[12] According to Frazier:

> The new Negro middle class . . . has a different economic base and a different social heritage from the relatively small middle class which had become differentiated from the masses of Negroes by the first decade of this century. This older middle class was an "aristocratic" *elite* in a sense because its social status and preeminence were based upon white ancestry and family and its behavior was modelled after the genteel tradition of the Old South. The upper layer derived their incomes from land but the majority of the members of the *"elite"* were employed in a large variety of occupations including positions as trusted retainers in white families. The new middle class has a different occupational basis and occupation is one of the important factors in determining status.[13]

This more differentiated stratification order, and emergent structure of hierarchical statuses, within the African American community can be perceived both as a response to the major social forces of the period and potentially as a weapon of mobilization for a subordinated minority group in a hostile environment. It should not be overlooked that such increased differentiation of the status structure within the African American community contributed to divisiveness and tensions or, as will be shown later, proved to be maladaptive for community solidarity.

A third adaptive response was the massive, almost sporadic, redistribution of the African American population within the United States. Often identified as The Great Migration, this movement is considered to have peaked around 1915 and involved both movement from rural to urban areas and dispersion from largely southern to other regions of the country.[14] It would be reasonable to expect profound effects, directly and indirectly, of this collective mobility upon those conditions influencing the process of social reorganization of the African American community and, as well, those linkages between it and significant groups and processes within American society.

The advent, by the end of the 1910–1920 decade, of a formal mass movement from the African American community is seen as a fourth adaptive response. Under the leadership of Marcus Garvey, the Universal Negro Improvement Association (U.N.I.A.) advanced a nationalist doctrine that allegedly captured, in particular, the imagination of the urban masses and working-class strata of the African American community. The Garvey Movement presented a provocative alternative to those tendencies within the African American community to accept the ideologies of, or the strategies for, interracialism, assimilation, and integration. This social movement signalled the presence of latent tensions and even resentments among significant elements of the social structure of the African American community. For example, among those caught in the African diaspora tensions existed among organizations, classes, regions, and disparate cultural groups such as the West Indians and the native African Americans.[15] At the same time, the Garvey Movement contributed to the development of collective identity, solidarity, and the idea of concerted action. Moreover, and most importantly, it contributed to the expansion or refocusing of perceptions about the experiences of injustice, inequality, and subordination of the African American community from a U.S. to a world perspective. Foster, in fact, called this social movement "a sort of Negro Zionism."[16]

The above profile permits the argument that between 1890 and 1919 the African American community was the singular object of, at the least, an implicit national policy of domination. This domination was malevolently fierce and demoniacal. It affected immediately, as well as cumulatively, all of the central elements of African American life in the United States, including identities, roles, and institutions. The consequences of this policy of domination was a despised but exploited minority community, stigmatized by alleged social inferiority, literally isolated from the legitimate sources of economic and political power, and largely excluded from the expectation of protection from the system of justice in a multiracial society paradoxically driven by an egalitarian ethic. American society could be viewed only as a hostile environment by the African American community.

It is reasonable to conclude, then, that the African American community during this particular period responded to its circumstances with a kind of defensive structuring.[17] This type of adaptation is observed regularly among groups (for example, the European Jewish communities) that see themselves as exposed to environmental stress of long duration with which they cannot cope directly and aggressively. Hence, defensive structuring permitted the African American community to generate a survival process for managing oppression and alienation while creating a collective consciousness suitable for engaging in concerted actions with allies for the purpose of liberation from inequality and injustice.

THE JEWISH AMERICAN COMMUNITY

Between approximately 1890 and 1919 the essential groundwork was in place for completion of the process of construction of the distinctive collective identity and consciousness of the Jewish American community. This groundwork entailed, fundamentally, an intense process of giving meanings to the particularity of singular features of the changing reality of American society and of world geopolitics. Thus, in 1896 Theodor Herzl published *Judenstaat* calling for the creation, preferably in Palestine, of an internationally recognized state.[18] On August 17, 1915, Leo M. Frank, a young married college graduate, the manager of a manufacturing establishment, and president of his local branch of B'nai B'rith, was lynched in Marietta, Georgia.[19] And in 1917 the Balfour Declaration pledging to the world British support for a Jewish national home in Palestine was announced.

A pervasive feature of the reality of this situation confronting, manifestly and latently, the emerging Jewish American community during this period was the mass immigration of European Jews to the United States. According to Lavender, 2,326,458 Jewish immigrants came from 1881 through 1924.[20] The period between 1890 and 1919 falls largely within the latter part of this European exodus to America (from about 1880 to 1914) or what Davidowicz calls The Great Jewish Migration of 1881 to 1914.[21]

Precisely during this period the United States was reaching the natural limits of its territorial expansion or closing the frontier; legitimating an ideological and political process whereby privileged groups (essentially

Anglo-Saxon Protestants) maintained and expanded their societal domination, thereby creating a distinctive hierarchy of stratification; bringing to an end the national policy of unlimited immigration; implementing or solidifying a policy of foreign conquest and imperialism; and legitimating the processes of exclusion of African Americans from democracy and justice.[22]

The immigration and settlement experiences in the United States of "the new Jewish immigrants," largely of Russian and Polish (or Eastern European) origin, during the last decade of the nineteenth and the first two decades of the twentieth centuries, have been well documented and vigorously studied.[23] This transformative experience of re-adaptation from the Old to the New World for these immigrants must have entailed an intense interplay of contrasting values, opportunities, and expectations. Without doubt this massive experience of acculturation, or "Americanization," as it was called colloquially, influenced profoundly both the emergent character of the Jewish American community — which until this period had been made up primarily of "the old Jewish immigrants" largely of Germanic (or Western European) origin — and that minority group's definition and role by all those otherwise making up American society.

An apt description of the general urban experiences of many of these immigrants is provided by August Wilson, 1987 Pulitzer Prize-winning playwright:

> Near the turn of the century, the destitute of Europe sprang on the city with tenacious claws and an honest and solid dream. The city devoured them. They swelled its belly until it burst into a thousand furnaces and sewing machines, a thousand butcher shops and baker's [sic] ovens, a thousand churches and hospitals and funeral parlors and money-lenders. The city grew. It nourished itself and offered each man a partnership limited only by his talent, his guile, and his willingness and capacity for hard work. For the immigrants of Europe, a dream dared and won true.[24]

The common view of American society held by the Jewish American community between 1890 and 1919 was influenced profoundly by contrasting it with the immediate, as well as historical, experiences of Jewish communities throughout the world, but especially in Europe. Thus, their prevailing view included both the expectation and promise of American ideological ideals — for example, religious, political, and civic freedoms — and a sense of liberation and freedom from their minority community or ghetto experiences among the nations of Europe. The Jewish American community had reason to believe that, grounded in feelings of solidarity derived from a common history and a community of fate as well as a community of faith, American society provided them the opportunity to become Americans and, at the same time, remain Jews.

A singular perception by the Jewish American community of the distinction between their minority status in America from that in the several European nations centered upon the principle of voluntarism. According to Davidowicz,

> In Europe, ... every Jew upon birth became a member of the Jewish community, a formal body with legal standing whose status was regulated by the government. ... To be a Jew then was a formal and legal ascription required by governing authorities. In America, in contrast, a Jew decided for himself freely and voluntarily whether he wished to associate himself with other Jews.[25]

However, this principle of voluntarism possessed hidden pitfalls for the emerging collective identity and consciousness of the Jewish American community. Ideally, by the individual exercise of the liberties of voluntarism a severe threat could be foreseen to the fundamental sources of collective solidarity so essential to the traditional Jewish polity. The acceptance of civic, political, and religious equality by members of the Jewish American community entailed simultaneously submitting to a process of adaptation and adjustment, even alienation, that could be costly to values traditionally held to be of paramount importance for group survival. Goal-directed behaviors and calculated strategies of action suggested rather precisely by the concepts of the melting pot or assimilation, integration, ethnic and cultural pluralism, and even nationalism became signal issues among the range of views about their environmental situation held between 1890 and 1920 by the Jewish American community.

This dominant view of American society — of promise and expectation, liberation and freedom — included also a malignant aspect. The social reality of America for the Jewish American community during this period meant also being vulnerable, individually and collectively, to bigotry and extralegal violence — lynchings, residential restrictions, professional and occupational discrimination and exclusion, and personal indignities. Thus, as with the African American community, the Jewish American community could perceive easily the barely disguised sinister attitude toward them regarding the essentiality, the fundamental characteristics, of American society. A sense of fear, of marginality, even alienation, from American society became an integral part of the existential reality of living in the United States for both the Jewish and the African American communities.

The record of hatred of the Jewish American, the ugly details of anti-Semitism in the United States, are well documented. Williams notes, illustratively:

> The historical record shows that the peaks in nativistic, ethnocentric sentiments and in overt discrimination and conflict came on the heels of periods of very large influx of visible different immigrants, or lagged behind only until the newcomers came into obvious and frequent competition with the "established" population. Anti-Jewish reactions are especially instructive. Until the 1840s such responses were relatively rare and mild. The rapid growth of a new German Jewish population evoked a sharp increase in negative attitudes. A second wave of anti-Jewish sentiment came in the 1870s and after, as upwardly mobile Jews came into competition with "possessors of privilege." And occupational and educational discrimination became widespread from about 1916.[26]

Thus, between about 1890 and 1919 the Jewish American community tended to perceive itself as being defined by American society as being a minority group both "different" and "competitive."

A pervasive ambiguity about group identity and perceived status for the Jewish American community grew out of the tensions between being defined in the United States generally as different and competitive and the American ideology — the expectations and promises — of freedom and equality. A fundamental issue of group survival was at stake here, given the undeniable presence of bigotry and extralegal violence. Resolution had to be made by the Jewish American community of the issues of "who" it was and "how" it should engage with others. That is, and this is of signal importance when compared with the plight of the African American community, this minority community had meaningful choices — assimilation, pluralism, separatism, or nationalism — in answering questions of identity and order. As a minority and subordinate group, the Jewish American community was compelled to come to grips with the establishing of relationships of similarity, difference, equality, and domination. Ways had to be evolved or constructed for establishing and maintaining internal order — discipline and solidarity — and the symbolic drawing of acceptable social boundaries between themselves and others. A consequence of this dilemma was the developmental emergence of a turbulent process of structural reorganization of the Jewish American community.

The reality and spirit of a central aspect of this process of structural change of the Jewish American community between 1890 and 1919 is captured well by Baltzell.[27] Against the background of increasing anti-Semitism, historical detail is provided of the processes of adjustment and accommodation made by the Jewish American community. Especially incisive is the descriptive analyses of those tensions, manifest and latent, and cleavages based upon cultural origin (Sephardic and Western European versus Russian, Polish, or Eastern European), caste, class, religion, and geographic concentration that characterized the dynamics of the Jewish American community during this period.

Two profoundly critical consequences followed the frenetic internal restructuring of the Jewish American community during this time period. First, there was the attainment of parity, if not superiority, of the Eastern European or "Russian Jews" with the Western European or "German Jews" in terms of control of the Jewish American community. No longer would the perceptions and definitions of Jewish interests in America be set or determined, almost unilaterally, by the descendants of the earlier arrived, assimilationist, and possibly more affluent sub-community of German Jews. The second critical consequence of the internal reorganization of the Jewish American community at this time was the effective legitimation of the Zionist movement — in all of its emotional, ideological, and nationalistic essence — as an essential component of the consciousness of the Jewish American community. These two developments will be seen to be of fateful significance in all efforts of the Jewish American community to ally with others.

Essentially, the Jewish American community, in defining its terms of being in the United States and identifying with its institutions, experienced profound structural change during this time. Its fundamental ideology and organizational characteristics were radically transformed out of the contradictions or conflicts between what may be called immigrant versus entrenched middleman minority strata.[28] Its status and privilege structures were adapted to accommodate diversity and heterogeneity; it moved from a familistic to a more formal and associational basis of communal organization — especially in the arenas of self-help, charity, and philanthropy; it accepted or was forced to begin to tolerate heterodoxy in matters of theological doctrine; it began to acquire the arts, crafts, and skills of successful competition in an open political system; and it judiciously tested and explored, on both local and national levels, the expediency of establishing alliances or coalitions.[29]

A reasonable argument therefore can be made that defensive structuring, as with the constructed response of the African American community, was the type of adaptation generally adopted by the Jewish American community to perceived American reality between 1890 and

1919. Refusing outright to trade in their traditional collective identity and self-consciousness, there are nevertheless signs that some numbers of the emergent Jewish American community tended to compromise primordial identity and forfeit elements of history. These indications include such commonly understood threats to group solidarity as intermarriage, name changing, and affiliation with various non-Jewish religious denominations.[30]

A collective response by the Jewish American community that was of utmost significance during this time was the adoption of the strategy of acquiring skill in exploiting the system of open politics in American cities. The Jewish American community understood well that collective survival, as well as the uncertainties of minority group status and the quality of relations with significant others, depended upon the ability to influence the state; and that this, in turn, depended on the location of its members in the productive process and the efficacy of their economic and political organizations. There was, therefore, an early collective awareness in the Jewish American community of the need to become positioned centrally and permanently within the essentially Anglo-Saxon Protestant arena of power,[31] and that this would lead to "life [being] sweeter in America than anywhere else in the world."[32]

MINORITY STATUS AND MUTUAL INTERESTS

Between 1890 and 1919 it would seem that a sense of acceptance began to be reached independently by the African and Jewish American communities about the substance of their core identities as minority groups among an essentially Anglo-Saxon Protestant majority. This beginning, clearly, was grounded deeply in the unique conjuncture of social forces operating at this particular time in the history of the United States. Both minority communities were stripped of their innocence in terms of the applicability to them then of the ideals and valuations of America; they had cruel knowledge of the implacable, indomitable, absolute definitions of them held by the American majority. Thus, the paramount tasks of both communities became that of defining carefully the situational reality of minority status and of constructing a way to cope with its particularity so as to insure their collective survival. Of vital significance, for both minority communities, were the differences in the United States between what things were and what they were said to be.

Nevertheless, while defined as minority groups in pluralistic American society, the African and Jewish American communities possessed uniqueness: at the least, in terms of collective goals and ideologies,

evolved cultural patterns, communal structures, relative size or magnitude, patterns of location or settlement, and general orientation toward or
involvement in foreign affairs. These two minority groups were not
perceived by members of the dominant majority as being identical or
interchangeable; nor did the members of the two minority groups tend to
define themselves as equals or their predicaments as being identical.

For, interestingly, there is some evidence that the African American
community tended generally to define Jewish Americans as "different and
competitive" in much the same way as did the dominant majority in
America; and, allegedly, this same tendency is discerned in the definition
of African Americans by the Jewish American community in much the
same way as by the dominant American majority. The particularistic
consciousness of the two minority communities, in other words, was
infected by the racist sentiments or ideology of the dominant American
society. Neither were these two minority communities controlled — that
is, constrained or limited — by the dominant majority in the same ways.
The realities of minority status, in other words, were not identical for the
African and Jewish American communities.

The ensemble of factors common to minority status within American
society for both the African and Jewish American communities involved
minimally isolation, ambiguity, alienation, exclusion, restriction, hostility, and fear. It is more difficult, however, to specify more precisely the
distinctions between the substance of minority status for the African and
Jewish American communities. What is crucial, nevertheless, is that the
two communities recognized, first, that within the context of American
society — essentially a configuration of social power involving collective
risk and uncertainty — they both were minority groups or marginal to the
dominant, essentially European-derived Anglo-Saxon Protestant majority
and, second, that the essentiality of their minority status was decidedly
unalike.

The stark and irreducible reality about the unlikeness of these two
minority communities (without addressing here the nature of their relative
size, settlement location, cultural and historical backgrounds, structural
organization, racial identity or perception, and human capital characteristics) is their perceived, situational, status nonequivalence within American society. In other words, in terms of the hierarchical organization of
racial and ethnic groups within the American social structure, the Jewish
American minority community occupied, or was accorded, a superior
status location, while the African American minority community occupied, or was accorded, an inferior status location. Any search, therefore,
for mutual group interests or opportunities of alliance and coalition

necessarily must be confounded by the inescapable facts that the African and Jewish American communities between approximately 1890 and 1919 were not equally situated in the American social structure, nor did they have parity as potential bargaining agents for agreeing upon and undertaking concerted action within the several power configurations of American society. Stated differently, bargaining between nonequals is inherently risky or, as the invading Athenians replied to the protesting islanders of Melos many millennia ago: "The strong do what they can and the weak suffer what they must."

Nevertheless, the process of recognizing the possibility of mutual collective interests between the African and Jewish American communities grew out of attempts to resolve the immediate consequences of pervasive hostility, inequality, injustice, poverty, and powerlessness particular for each minority community. Both accepted the utter futility of the alternative of mounting resistance-type movements within the United States and rejected as largely unreasonable the alternative of group emigration such as may have been implicit within the Garvey and Zionist movements. The mobilizing of each community, for what I earlier called defensive structuring, fundamentally involved the construction of collective identity, consciousness and group unity or solidarity, and a constant search for possible allies.

The educational system, or the institution of public schooling, was perceived throughout the time between 1890 and 1919 as a nonthreatening arena for concerted action by the African and Jewish American communities. For both minority communities formal schooling was identified as a major means for influencing their survival in America and for controlling the effects of being defined as apart from and different from the dominant European-derived Anglo-Saxon Protestant majority. The entire public school system for the African American community — legally as well as in terms of common practice and, generally, in non-southern as well as southern locations — was organized separate from and unequal to the public schooling system of all other Americans (with the possible exception of Native Americans residing on reservations). The devastating effects of this arrangement, cumulatively transmitted and enhanced throughout subsequent generational cohorts, are being felt to this day by American society. This infamous schooling arrangement — separate and unequal — ordinarily was not experienced by the Jewish American or other minority communities in the United States.

Beyond this pervasive structural characteristic of racist separation in public schooling, and complicating the search of the African and Jewish American communities for alliances and allies, the institution of education remained in a state of continual tension responding to social forces over which it had little control.[33] During the last quarter of the nineteenth century, for instance, great controversy emerged among educators, politicians, and policy makers about who was to be schooled and what was to be the substance of this schooling. As another instance, major attempts were made in the decades preceding and following the turn of the century to increase the competencies of the several cadres of professionals serving the various levels of the public educational system. At the same time the public school system was racked by fierce struggles, largely concentrated in the metropolitan areas of the nation, over who was to exercise control.

It may be fair to say that during this crucial time for the cultivating of allies and the arranging of alliances by these two minority communities the educational system was an object of intense struggle by powerful national interests. What was at stake here essentially was domination of the institution of public schooling considered as the bastion of knowledge or cultural capital. At stake also was that instrumentality in American society central to the acquisition and maintenance of group power, control, and privilege.

Relations within the educational system between the African and Jewish American communities at this time were played out largely through the advent of the movement of philanthropy in the United States. Neither a public, governmental, nor commercial, profit-making sphere, this third sector, philanthropy, is best thought of as a constellation of private institutions disposing of private funds allegedly, on the manifest level, for the discovery and the resolving of social problems.[34] The schooling of African Americans, as a central element of the national policy of racial domination, was seen almost universally as such a social problem.

As operative agencies of the philanthropic movement, foundations exerted tremendous influence on the character of education for African Americans, according to Bullock.[35] They accepted the quiet, nonpublic decisions reached by those attending the famous Capon Springs, West Virginia, conferences — the first was convened in June 1898 — of the appropriateness of a special kind of schooling (Industrial Education) for African Americans. These quiet, nonpublic decisions — in which the basic collective interests and constitutional rights of African Americans were sacrificed without their decisive and meaningful participation — contributed to a policy consensus for philanthropic action. They were reached by decision makers and power brokers from the North and from the South who were determined to maintain European American hegemony throughout the nation as part of the ideology of racial superiority. Race separation and an invidious and pernicious pattern of gross inequity of educational resources and opportunities for African and European American schooling were salient features of this policy consensus legitimated in part by American philanthropy.

Sensitive to criticism of the ethical grounds upon which the conduct of American industry operated and in response to massive changes transforming the economic and industrial character of the nation, wealthy individuals such as Andrew Carnegie, John D. Rockefeller, George Peabody, and John F. Slater along with, from the Jewish American community, Julius Rosenwald, Jacob Schiff, and Felix Warburg[36] initially provided the finances for philanthropic involvement with issues of race and education.

With this recognition, however, of the national scope of the problem of African American education, according to Diner,[37] the Jewish American philanthropists assumed what appeared to be contradictory roles with respect to the European-derived Anglo-Saxon Protestant majority, the African American community, and the masses of the Jewish American community. They seemed to accept, generally, the racist ideology of the European American philanthropists and yet, simultaneously, legitimated acceptance by the Jewish American community of the African American community — which exhibited some resistance to the dominant racist educational ideology — as an ally. In other words, it would seem that the philanthropic elite of the Jewish American community was in accord with the philanthropic elite interests of the dominant majority and, at the same time, aided, abetted, and avidly supported financially the educational and intellectual elites of the African American community.

Motivations underpinning this apparently generalized role of the Jewish American community are hard to come by. Maybe the puzzle is understandable if one assumes it was motivated both by the urge felt by the Jewish American community to assimilate, accommodate, and survive and by the centrality of the values of charity and education in the subculture of the Jewish American community.

The dynamics of partnership roles within the emergent alliance between these two minority communities are singular: on the one hand in terms of interactive structure and quality and on the other hand in terms of possible outcomes. The African and Jewish American communities were not consciously engaged interactively as equal partners in a common cause.[38] Rather, the intergroup relationship involved manifestly the complementary roles of askers and givers. Little evidence is at hand to suggest that attention was paid by any of the acting parties to the possible unhealthy consequences of philanthropy upon the receivers. The Jewish American community assumed, essentially, the role of broker for the African American community to the dominant European American majority. Action aspects of this brokerage role involved, for the Jewish American community, sets of behavior identified with interpreter, intermediary, and champion.[39]

The almost unanimously observed patent inequality of this initial decision-making process of these fumbling allies was compromised by at least two considerations. First, there was the apparent acceptance of the alleged merits of the existing educational situation for the African American community, and, second, there were implicit expectations or consequences for the ideological objectives and the status position of the Jewish American community in their linkages with dominant European American elites. Thus, in view of the apparently unequal yoking of these emergent partners, and motivated largely by the paramount survival concerns of the Jewish American community, it is not amiss to speculate that at least within the educational domain the potentialities of the African American community may have been bargained as a negotiable power of exchange by the Jewish American elite.[40]

Another arena, ripe at this time for alliance between the African and Jewish American communities, was the legal and civil rights domain. The policies of oppression, exclusion, persecution, and pervasive dehumanization implemented against African Americans in the United States was a frightful spectacle to the Jewish American community given their collective experiences as well as historical knowledge of intergroup intolerance and bigotry. The Jewish American community was alarmed especially by such incidents as the exclusion in 1870 of Joseph Seligman from the Grand Union Hotel in Saratoga Springs, New York, the lynching of Leo Frank in 1915, the exclusion from Harvard University of Roscoe Conklin Bruce, the Savage Affair in Augusta, Georgia, and the Cohen controversy in New Orleans.[41] It was prudent for the Jewish American community, therefore, to interpret these portents as possibly signalling a redirecting or widening of the scope in America of those racist policies heretofore limited largely to the African American community.

The legal status of those of African descent has been a persistent and largely intractable problem for the United States.[42] It seems to be fairly certain that in the attempts of the African American community to manage this racking problem the Jewish American community earned recognition or began to be clearly perceived as a potential ally during those critical decades between 1890 and 1920. It was during this period that the African American community undertook seriously the creation of organizations concerned essentially with agendas to pay attention to legal status and civil rights, employment, education, and welfare; the cultivation of the development of leadership; and connections with private and governmental agencies.[43]

The participation of and the roles performed by members of the Jewish American community in the origination and subsequent development of those instruments of defensive structuring — especially the NAACP and the National Urban League — have been well documented.[44]

The ambiguous and even controversial interrelationship of the Jewish and African American communities in this domain of legal and civil rights has been described cogently by Reed.[45] He argues that there were several types of relationships, rather than a single one, between representatives of the two minority communities and that the essentiality of the relationships was determined "through the mediation of elite-driven formal advocacy organizations such as the NAACP and the National Urban League on the one side and the American Jewish Congress, American Jewish Committee, and Anti-Defamation League of B'nai B'rith on the other."[46] He pointedly comments upon the advantages conferred by the dual status of Jewish Americans in the dynamics of the "mediated interaction" between the two minority communities.[47]

The relations of the African and Jewish American communities in that social policy arena involving issues of economics and social services merit much more careful examination than they have received. Efforts at articulation of strategies for concerted actions involving issues of economics and social welfare services by the two minority communities during this time were complicated by their distinct situational realities within American society. These differences of situation included, at the least, structural inequalities in manpower utilization patterns within the economic order, differences in mastery of the perplexities of urban or metropolitan politics, and the relative status or positions of power on the national level of their respective elite structures.

Put simply, the immediate existential reality for the two minority communities were unalike. Dissimilarities existed in terms of such essentials as work opportunity, social status and security, educational attainment, financial status, health, problems of individual and collective welfare, and the short- and long-run ideological orientations (that is, pluralism, accommodation, assimilation, and nationalism) of the African and Jewish American communities.

Alliance and coalition relationships — the sharing of power — between the African and Jewish American communities in the arena of economics and social services are nearly invisible during the last decade of the nineteenth century and the first two decades of the twentieth century. As workers those making up the African American community were fearfully exploited both by employers and by the organized labor movement through a pervasive pattern of systemic discrimination, segregation, inequality, exclusion, and even terror and violence.[48] This work-force experience of systematic restriction and exploitation, inequity, fear, and disillusion was not shared in the same way or in like degree by members of the Jewish American community. Some efforts (for example, unionization and employee recruitment) at concerted action and cooperation between the two minority communities, nevertheless, were made.[49]

That inexorably enduring issue of the relative importance of class and race in minority group relations surfaced during this time among organized labor organizations and political factions and parties.[50] The inability to resolve this issue of the primacy of race or class in racial and ethnic group relations permeated the reform activities emerging during this time in the causes of labor and class justice. The intractability of this issue for the formation of alliances between the African and Jewish American communities is evident throughout their participation in the Settlement House and Social Gospel Movements and in the emergence of the so-called radicalism of the new Liberalism and the New Social Science.[51] Essentially, the involvement of the African American community in these arenas of ideological ferment and reform activities may be characterized as marginal and indirect, while that of the Jewish American community is best described as central and direct. Perhaps the intrinsic marginality and dependency of the African American community, as well as its stigmatized status within the hierarchy of minority groups perceived as constituting American society, combined to impede the development of an effective coalescence with the Jewish American community.

A most curious situation existed in terms of alliance and coalition between the African and Jewish American communities in the politics of power. African Americans at this time were burdened, uniquely among minority groups in the United States, by the reality that the laws and practices governing political participation — in violation of the explicit and implicit canons of representative democracy and constitutionalism — almost completely disenfranchised them. Both minority communities doubtless understood pragmatically such principles of the power of politics as like-minded interests of minority groups, rather than individual citizens, as the backbone of power politics; the unwillingness of citizens generally to tyrannize themselves; the coalitions of interest groups thatform and re-form as different issues arise, or that political cleavages are seldom cumulative; and the elected officials (politicians) who frequently transform their own, rather than their constituents', wishes into public policy.[52] Fundamentally, however, neither minority community seemed to realize the limits that the fact of race placed on practical power politics in the United States.

From the viewpoint of the African American community at this time, and regardless of how the politics of power are perceived, the ultimate division in the United States always was race. Given the human propensity to view one's own problems as very serious, this viewpoint may be accepted as a reasonable collective position. However, history and experience tend to tilt toward supporting the view that class, occupation, region, gender, religion, or political interest submitted always to race. A result during this period was the emergence throughout the African American community of what has been called the "mugwump" style of European-derived Anglo-Saxon Protestant politics.[53]

The central ingredients of this style involved progressive sentiments added to a central preoccupation with race relations. Generally speaking, the African American community seemed to have little serious interest in the organization of precincts and diligent vote solicitation that could produce the solid constituencies required to compete for and capture political power. Under the mugwump umbrella the leadership style of the African American community tended to feature a reliance upon the moral obligation that patrons, national leaders, and other interested individuals or groups could be made to feel about the race issue. This mode of leadership seemed to contrast sharply with a style designed, as in the Irish, Italian, German, Polish, and Jewish American communities, to create the kind of political organizations that could effectively capture and control power or create a political base. Finally, a visible tendency emerged in the African American community to look for protection and relief in political matters to the federal government rather than to the state and local governments. This tendency continues to this day, and remnants remain of this collective response of ardent support of federal control and extension of federal power.

The Jewish American community, between approximately 1890 and 1919, had an approach to social policy issues in the arenas of economics and social services that was largely free of perversions of the canons of representative democracy and constitutionalism and, therefore, was quite unlike the approach of the African American community. Critical issues of internal cleavage and discord had been resolved with the ascendancy of the Russian Jew to apparent dominance in the Jewish American community, and a role for involvement in the foreign affairs of the nation had been provided by the legitimation of modern Zionism as an essential agenda item of the Jewish American community. Lavender provides a useful overview of the approach of the Jewish American community with the situational context not only permitting but rewarding individual and group accommodation, assimilation, and mobility within which it was embedded.[54]

Again, and without the limitations experienced by the African American community, the intricacies of the pluralistic grounding of the politics of power within urban contexts were early mastered by the Jewish American community. The "fondness for socialism" of the Jewish American community during this period has been observed[55] and, out of this heritage of political organization and activism, early attempts were made to ally, among others, with the African American community.

For deeper understanding of the efforts at alliance and coalition between the African and Jewish American communities during this time period, even though primary sources are literally nonexistent, closer analysis of the relative status of their respective elite structure is needed. Clearly, those African Americans who were able through their positions in relatively influential and visible organizations to affect national political outcomes regularly and seriously were few and relatively powerless when compared with representatives of the Jewish American community. Furthermore, it is very likely that the amalgam of attitudes, values, and interpersonal relations among those factors making up the African and Jewish American communities — the nature of their elite structures — was dissimilar.[56]

It would seem that the elite structures of these minority communities did not conform to what in classical elite theory is labeled a totalitarian, monocratic, or ideologically unified type. Nor could they be easily and accurately described as being either a divided, competitive, or disunified elite structure or a pluralistic, competitive-coalescent, or consensually unified elite structure.[57] Dissimilarity of minority community elite structure of itself is not important; the issue is how such differing characteristics operate in that process of bargaining, negotiating, cooperating, and conflicting about what to engage in preliminary to alliance and coalition.

Before going on to examine, in subsequent chapters, the continuing interrelations of the African and Jewish American communities during succeeding time periods in twentieth-century America, it can be fairly said now that from approximately 1890 to 1919 there was mutual recognition by both minority communities of a common peril in the United States. In attempting to share with equity in that promise of the nation's values they agreed generally in identifying their ultimate antagonist as, in the main, the European-derived Anglo-Saxon Protestant majority. From these considerations, at least, there is evidence of some efforts by the African and Jewish American communities to plan, cooperate, and act together in major arenas of social policy and problems.

The process and the consequences of these early efforts remain to be illuminated more fully in later sections of this work. At this point what is remarkable in this very summary description of the initial phase of alliance and coalition building between the African and Jewish American communities is their situational dissimilarity within American society. Simply put, as minority communities they did not begin to interact as equal entities within the social power realities of American society.

Their relative social status as well as structural inequality, preliminary to beginning the process of becoming allies, is manifest in terms of articulation with their definition and perception by the greater American society. All of the evidence suggests that the African American community occupied a bargaining position of subordination and inferiority. The terms of the condition of minority status and dependency of the African and Jewish American communities are starkly unalike. Their collective postures in the existential reality of power, control, and domination within American society at this particular time is starkly more dissimilar than similar with respect to both essential ends (pluralism, assimilation, integration) and essential means (constitutional legalism and mastery of the politics of power). The general posture, then, of the African American community toward domination and power somehow brings to mind the description of the Aztec people following their conquest and ravaging by the Spanish as found in that classic history of race and culture by Prescott[58] — "But ages of tyranny have passed over him; he belongs to a conquered race."

Moreover, any comparative assessment of those human capital resources associated with the organizational structures of the two minority communities, and especially those considered to be essential for alliance or coalition success, seems to be tilted always to the advantage of the Jewish American community. Further examination should reveal whether these observations about the character of early attempts at alliance and coalition by these two minority communities are to be transmitted as a kind of legacy.

NOTES

1. Benjamin Quarles, *The Negro in the Making of America* (New York: Collier Books, 1968), pp. 141–42. William Z. Foster, *The Negro People in American History* (New York: International Publishers, 1970), pp. 335–44.

2. See Foster, *The Negro People*, p. 393.

3. See Quarles, *The Negro in the Making of America*, pp. 144–47; and especially, Foster, *The Negro People*, pp. 376–96.

4. Saunders Redding, *The Lonesome Road* (New York: Dolphin Books, 1958), pp. 83–91. For an exhaustive treatment of this topic see Bernard C. Nalty, *Strength for the Fight: A History of Black Americans in the Military* (New York: Free Press, 1986), Chapter 5, pp. 63–77.

5. Sixty-six years later, in 1972, the federal government, conceding its error and accepting responsibility for subsequent injustices, reversed its decisions and attempted to make restitution for damages to the single survivor. See the saga of Dorsie W. Willis in articles of *The New York Times* of December 31, 1972, p. 33N; February 8, 1977, p. 33; and August 25, 1977, p. 2B. More scholarly treatment of this incident is to be found in Kelly Miller, *Radicals and Conservatives and Other Essays on the Negro in America* (New York: Schocken Books, 1968), pp. 307–20; Redding, *The Lonesome Road*, pp. 198–99; Ann J. Lane, *The Brownsville Affair: National Crisis and Black Reaction* (Port Washington, NY: Kennikat Press, 1971); and Nalty, *Strength for the Fight*, Chapter 7, pp. 87–106.

6. Foster, *The Negro People*, pp. 420–21. Also, for a comprehensive examination of the 1906 Atlanta riots and of race relations in America at this time, see Miller, *Radicals and Conservatives*, pp. 71–101.

7. Gunnar Myrdal, *An American Dilemma: The Negro Problem and Modern Democracy* (New York: Harper & Brothers, 1944), pp. 745–50. The orally transmitted accounts of my uncle — Frank Jasper Williamson, who served for more than a year in the United States and in France as a member of "Pioneer" Infantry Company "M" of the U.S. Army and was honorably discharged on June 18, 1919 — support the accounts of these dismal experiences and constitute an integral part of my familial heritage.

8. Foster, *The Negro People*, p. 435.

9. Quarles, *The Negro in the Making of America*, pp. 192–93. For an especially detailed coverage of "the Red Summer of 1919," see Nalty, *Strength for the Fight*, pp. 125–42.

10. There is a massive body of literature dealing with this issue. I have found very helpful Miller, *Radicals and Conservatives*, pp. 25–41; Louis R. Harlan, *Booker T. Washington: The Making of a Black Leader, 1856–1901* (New York: Oxford, 1972); Louis R. Harlan, *Booker T. Washington: The Wizard of Tuskegee, 1901–1915* (New York: Oxford, 1983); Emmett J. Scott and Lyman B. Stowe, *Booker T. Washington: Builder of a Civilization* (New York: Doubleday, Page & Co., 1916); and Foster, *The Negro People*, pp. 408–18.

11. See especially E. Franklin Frazier, *The Negro Church in America* (New York: Schocken Books, 1963); Myrdal, *An American Dilemma*, especially Chapter 43; Foster, *The Negro People*, pp. 393–429; Charles H. Wesley, *History of Sigma Pi Phi: First of the Negro-American Greek Letter Fraternities* (Washington, DC: Association for the Study of Negro Life and History, 1969), Chapters I and II; and

William A. Muraskin, *Middle-Class Blacks in a White Society: Prince Hall Masonry in America* (Berkeley: University of California Press, 1975). A detailed examination of the role of the African American press, at this particular time, in the mobilization of the African American community against racism is found in Enoch P. Waters, *American Diary: A Personal History of The Black Press* (Chicago: Path Press, 1983).

12. Redding, *The Lonesome Road*, p. 195.

13. Frazier, *The Negro Church in America*, pp. 76–77.

14. Myrdal, *An American Dilemma*, Chapter 8 and pp. 191–201. Also, see Foster, *The Negro People*, pp. 437–39.

15. The dynamics of the social strata within a minority group such as the African American community deserves scholarly attention in its own right. The African American community is not a monolithic social aggregation. Constant strains, cleavages, and tensions between the diverse elements making up this community based upon skin color, cultural origin, family background, spatial (that is, urban, rural, regional, and sectional) location, politics and ideology, religion, occupation and profession, educational attainment, and styles of life have been well documented. For some examples of analyses of such intragroup dynamics see Harold Cruse, *Plural but Equal* (New York: W. Morrow, 1987), pp. 299–342; Rudolph Fisher, *The Walls of Jericho* (New York: Arno Press, 1969); Robert J. Norrell, *Reaping the Whirlwind: The Civil Rights Movement in Tuskegee* (New York: Knopf, 1985); Adolph L. Reed, Jr., "Black Particularity Reconsidered," *Telos* 30 (Spring 1979): 71–94; and Muraskin, *Middle-Class Blacks*, pp. 83–85.

16. Foster, *The Negro People*, p. 450. See also pp. 442–51. Much has been written about this social movement. Of unusual value are John M. Clarke, *Marcus Garvey* (New York: Vintage Books, 1974); Cruse, *The Crisis of the Negro Intellectual* (New York: Morrow, 1967); Edmund D. Cronon, *Black Moses* (Madison: University of Wisconsin Press, 1969); and Myrdal, *An American Dilemma*, pp. 746–48.

17. See Bernard J. Siegel, "Defensive Structuring and Environmental Stress," *American Journal of Socioloty* 76:1 (July 1970): 11–21.

18. Hollis R. Lynch, *Edward Wilmot Blyden: Pan-Negro Patriot* (London: Oxford University Press, 1970), p. 64.

19. Cruse, *Plural but Equal*, p. 479; and David Levering Lewis, *When Harlem Was in Vogue* (New York: Knopf, 1981), p. 547. Feuerlicht observes that "Between 1889 and 1918, over 2,500 blacks were lynched. During that period, one Jew was lynched, Leo Frank in Georgia." See Roberta Strauss Feuerlicht, *The Fates of the Jews* (New York: Times Books, 1983), p. 188. The most extensive treatment found of the Frank lynching is in Gustavus Myers, *History of Bigotry in the United States* (New York: Capricorn Books, 1960), pp. 202–6. The epilogue of this lynching, according to *The New York Times* of March 16, 1986, p. 6, was the awarding of a posthumous pardon by the State of Georgia to Leo M. Frank for the crime that allegedly led to the lynching. According to Davis, the first recorded Jewish victim of a lynching is S. A. Bierfeld of Franklin, Tennessee, in 1868. See Lenwood G. Davis, *Black-Jewish Relations in the United States, 1752–1984* (Westport, CT: Greenwood Press, 1984), p. xi.

20. Abraham D. Lavender, *A Coat of Many Colors* (Westport, CT: Greenwood Press, 1977), p. 7.

21. Davidowicz, *A Century of Jewish History*, pp. 3–98.

22. For an incisive analysis of these societal processes and their interconnection, see especially Part II, pp. 43–114 of Hans J. Morgenthau, *The Purpose of American Politics* (New York: Knopf, 1960).

23. I have found the following materials useful as an introduction to this general area: E. Digby Baltzell, *The Protestant Establishment* (New York: Vintage Books, 1964), especially Chapter III; Davidowicz, *A Century of Jewish History*, 1981; Hasia R. Diner, *In the Almost Promised Land: American Jews and Blacks, 1915–1935* (Westport, CT: Greenwood Press, 1977); Feuerlicht, *Fates of the Jews*, 1983; Richard D. Hecht, "The Face of Modern Anti-Semitism," *The Center Magazine* XIV:2 (March/April 1981): 17–36; Lavender, *A Coat of Many Colors*, 1977; Marshall Sklare, "The Jews At Home In The City," *Commentary* (April 1972): 70–77; Wirth, *The Ghetto*, 1956; and Robert G. Weisbord and Arthur Stein, *Bittersweet Encounter: The Afro-American and The American Jew* (Westport, CT: Negro Universities Press, 1970).

24. August Wilson, "Preface to Fences," *Playbill*. 87:4 (April 1987): 26. Wilson then continues by describing, in a devastatingly instructive comparison, the identical situational setting for African Americans:

> The descendants of African slaves were offered no such welcome or participation. They came from places called the Carolinas and the Virginias, Georgia, Alabama, Mississippi, and Tennessee. They came strong, eager, searching. The city rejected them and they fled and settled along the riverbanks and under bridges in shallow, ramshackle houses made of sticks and tarpaper. They collected rags and wood. They sold the use of their muscles and their bodies. They cleaned houses and washed clothes, they shined shoes, and in quiet desperation and vengeful pride, they stole, and lived in pursuit of their own dream; that they could breathe free, finally, and stand to meet life with the force of dignity and whatever eloquence the heart could call upon.

25. Davidowicz, *A Century of Jewish History*, pp. 21–22. Also see Daniel J. Elazer, *Community and Polity* (Philadelphia: Jewish Publication Society of America, 1976), pp. 6–7.

26. Robin M. Williams, *Mutual Accommodation: Ethnic Conflict and Cooperation* (Minneapolis: University of Minnesota Press, 1977), p. 394. For analyses and accounts of various aspects of the cyclical waves of bigotry and extralegal violence against the Jewish American see Baltzell, *The Protestant Establishment*, pp. 58–59; Myers, *History of Bigotry in the United States*, especially Chapters XIX–XXIV; Marcia Graham Synnott, *The Half-Opened Door: Discrimination and Admission at Harvard, Yale, and Princeton, 1900–1970* (Westport, CT: Greenwood Press, 1979); Sklare, "The Jews At Home In The City," 1972; Davidowicz, *A Century of Jewish History*, 1981; Weisbord & Stein, *Bittersweet Encounter*, 1970; Feuerlicht, *Fates of the Jews*, 1983; and Hecht, *Face of Modern Anti-Semitism*, pp. 17–36.

27. Baltzell, *Protestnat Establishment*, Chapter III, but especially pp. 58–60. See also Davidowicz, *A Century of Jewish History*, pp. 3–31. For a description of the concerted positions and actions taken by many of the influential Jewish leaders (for example, Felix Warburg, Jacob Schiff, Oscar Straus, Mayer Sulzberger, Otto Kahn, the Seligmans, Louis D. Brandeis, Felix Adler, and the

Lehmans) see Diner, *In the Almost Promised Land*, 1977; and Sklare, *The Jews at Home*, 1972.

28. For an excellent treatment of theories of middleman minorities see Edna Bonacich, "A Theory of Middleman Minorities," *American Sociological Review* 38 (1973): 583–94; Walter Zenner, *Middleman Minority Theories and the Jews* (New York: YIVO, 1978); and H. M. Blalock, Jr., *Toward a Theory of Minority-Group Relations* (New York: John Wiley & Sons, 1967), pp. 79–84. The middle man minority role emerges worldwide, it seems, from two major conditions: discrimination and hostility, and the assumption of selected functional requisities.

29. There has been much attention paid to examples of these dynamics of the Jewish American community between 1890 and 1920. Of much help to me were Berson, *Negroes and the Jews*, 1971; Davidowicz, *A Century of Jewish History*, 1981; Diner, *In the Almost Promised Land*, 1977; Elazar, *Community and Polity*, 1976; Eli N. Evans, *The Provincials: A Personal History of Jews in the South* (New York: Athenaeum, 1974); Feuerlicht, *Fates of the Jews*, 1983; Paul Johnson, *A History of the Jews* (New York: Harper & Row, 1987); Weisbord & Stein, *Bittersweet Encounter*, 1970; and Synnott, *Half-Opened Door*, 1974.

30. For a cogent introduction to matters of exogamy, forfeiting of history, compromising of identity, and other such strategies, see the foreword of Weisbord & Stein, *Bittersweet Encounter*, 1970.

31. This idea is introduced and developed fairly completely in Johnson, *History of the Jews*, 1987. See, for example, pp. 279–82.

32. Weisbord & Stein, *Bittersweet Encounter*, p. xiv.

33. For historical treatments of school reform during this time period see Lawrence Cremin, *The Transformation of the School* (New York: Knopf, 1961); Michael Katz, *The Irony of Early School Reform* (Boston: Beacon Press, 1970); and Carter G. Woodson, *The Mis-Education of the Negro* (Washington, DC: Associated Publishers, 1933).

34. For an excellent treatment of foundations and philanthropy see James Douglas & Aaron Wildavsky, *The Future and the Past: Essays on Programs and the Annual Report, 1976–77* (New York: Russell Sage Foundation, 1977), pp. 19–24.

35. Henry Allen Bullock, *A History of Negro Education in the South* (New York: Praeger, 1970). See especially pp. 89–146.

36. Diner, *In the Almost Promised Land*, pp. 154–57.

37. Ibid., pp. 154–75.

38. Feuerlicht, *Fates of the Jews*, pp. 186–87. One common agreement among almost all who study this topic closely must be noted here; it will be explored more fully in later chapters. This consensus is about the apparent lack of parity, or the inequality, characterizing the "collaboration," "mediated interaction," "brokering," "the bittersweet encounters," "bonds of empathy," or "concerted actions" observed to make up a major dimension of the relationship between these African American and Jewish American allies.

39. See the section entitled "The Bonds of Empathy" in Diner, *In the Almost Promised Land*, 1977.

40. See the section entitled "To Serve At The Common Altar: Jews and Black Philanthropy" in Diner, *In the Almost Promised Land*; and Bullock, *History of Negro Education*, especially pp. 89–146.

41. Diner, *In the Almost Promised Land,* p. 100; and Berson, *Negroes and the Jews,* p. 53.

42. For a trenchant overview of this see Kenneth S. Tollett, "What Led to Bakke," *The Center Magazine* XI:1 (January/February 1978): 2.

43. See Sethard Fisher, "Black Americans Need Their Own Agenda," *The Center Magazine* 20:3 (May/June 1987): 26.

44. See David Levering Lewis, "Parallels and Divergences: Assimilationist Strategies of Afro-American and Jewish Elites from 1910 to the Early 1930s," *The Journal of American History* 71 (December 1984); Diner, *In the Almost Promised Land*; and Davidowicz, *A Century of Jewish History.* A summary description of the origin, general mission, tactics, and contributions to civil rights of the NAACP may be found in Blackwell, *The Black Community,* pp. 195–96.

45. Adolph L. Reed, Jr., *The Jesse Jackson Phenomenon* (New Haven: Yale University Press, 1986), pp. 88–105.

46. Ibid., p. 89.

47. Ibid., pp. 89–90. According to Reed, the Jewish American community

has at least two advantages in this mediated interaction. Because the interaction has been largely governed by an ideological commitment to interracialism, Jews have been able to steer "dialogue" from each side, both as representatives of autonomous Jewish interest groups and as prominent forces within interracial civil rights organizations. The peculiarity of Jewishness as a status that is neither racial, nor national nor, for that matter, necessarily religious exonerates Jewish elites from the imperative of organizational interracialism in their own domain while demanding obeisance to it from black civil rights organizations.

48. Foster, *The Negro People,* pp. 426–27

49. Diner, *In the Almost Promised Land,* p. 203.

50. Foster, *The Negro People,* especially Chapter 37: "The Socialists and the Negro People," pp. 397–407, 408–41.

51. Baltzell, *Protestant Establishment,* pp. 179–271.

52. Walter F. Murphy, "The Constitution and the 14th Amendment," *The Center Magazine* 20:4 (July/August 1987): 9–30.

53. Nathan I. Huggins, "Afro-Americans: National Character and Community," *The Center Magazine* VII:4 (July/August 1974): 51–66.

54. Lavender, *A Coat of Many Colors*; see the introduction, but especially pp. 10–12.

55. Feuerlicht, *Fates of the Jews,* pp. 117–20. Also see Foster, *The Negro People,* especially Chapter 37, pp. 397–407.

56. Lewis, *When Harlem Was in Vogue.*

57. Michael G. Burton & John Higley, "Elite Settlements," *American Sociological Review* 52:3 (June 1987): 296–97.

58. William H. Prescott, *History of the Conquest of Mexico & History of the Conquest of Peru* (New York: Modern Library, n.d.), p. 34.

3

Between World Wars

The 1920s has been described from diverse perspectives. One such view saw these years as the beginning of the modern world or, again, the epitome of the new age. The essential message of this time was "the world is not what it seems to be." The singular feature of the 1920s, according to this perspective, crystallized out of the convergence of Freudianism, Marxism, the "death of God" and "will to power" ideology of Nietzsche, and Einstein's general theory of relativity.[1]

Throughout the world then, as always, the idea systems of an older social and cultural order were being discarded helter-skelter and other sets of ideologies and paradigms were being authenticated and legitimated. For example, the breaking up of the European system of dynastic, proprietary, and monarchical empires entailed its replacement with the principle of self-determinism (that is, the adjustment of state or national frontiers by plebiscite according to ethnic and racial preferences). Out of the intricacies of this ferment of change in the old social and cultural order, in turn, came an essential part of the background for the Balfour Declaration. This 1917 declaration promised what was essentially the European Jewish community a national home in Palestine in return for deserting the Central Powers (principally Germany, Austria-Hungary, Turkey, and Russia) of World War I and aligning themselves with the Western Allies (principally the British Empire, France, and the United States).[2]

Under the canopy of the above selective European — if not worldwide — changes and in tune with the essential message, the United States had to deal at least with the nationwide changes wrought by the economic and cultural renaissance of the 1920s, the advent of communism, and the Great Depression of the 1930s. While allegedly continuing to become a liberal pluralist state, the nation in the 1920s and 1930s clearly began to assume that domestic interventionist stance that would lead the way into the New Deal, the New Frontier, and the Great Society of future decades. For, in general, one effect of the above worldwide changes (and especially of World War I) upon all nation-states was to increase their sizes and, therefore, their destructive capacities and propensities to oppress.[3] Thus, within the scope of these sets of worldwide and domestic changes are to be interpreted the negotiating, bargaining, cooperating, and conflicting relations of the African and Jewish American communities between World Wars I and II.

The observation was made in the previous chapter that some distinct features become evident as a part of the process of alliance or coalition formation between these two minority communities prior to 1920. Both the African and Jewish American communities had come to recognize, and had accepted tacitly, their mutual peril as minority groups in American society. They had come to see, too, the possible benefits of alliance and coalition for their common survival possibilities in the United States. The situational dissimilarities and relative social status of the two minority communities with respect to collective or group inequality and dependency within American society was at least implicitly appreciated. In addition, as previously indicated, some evidence suggested that the organizational structures of the two minority communities were evolving along different paths, the Jewish American path toward complete acceptance if not assimilation, and the African American path toward continued inferiority or stigmatized acceptance, subordinated, and pariah status. Finally, it is not clear whether the African and Jewish American communities held compatible views of either their ultimate collective goals (that is, some form of pluralism, nationalism, or assimilation) or of the requisite means for survival in essentially a European-derived Anglo-Saxon Protestant-dominated American society.

The Jewish American community, for instance, was not immediately threatened by such imperatives as legal discrimination, political disenfranchisement, and endemic poverty. And, obversely, the African American community, apart from the transient and episodic flirtation with the so-called Black Nationalism of Marcus Garvey, was not overwhelmingly caught up with the contradictory implications of issues such as assimilation, acculturation, integration, and Americanization implacably implicit within such movements as Zionism. Regardless of these apparent dissimilarities, however, both minority communities knew that they needed each other as allies.

In what follows in this chapter, the alliance or coalition formation process between these two minority communities during the 1920s and 1930s is deduced by observing exploratively how they responded jointly to several sets of national experiences. These are the "Red Scare" and the rise of bigotry and anti-Semitism; the evolving character of formally organized African leadership, the meanings of the Harlem Renaissance and, most significantly, the complicated role of the Communist Party in the struggle for racial equality and justice; and the Great Depression.

THE RED SCARE

What is called the Red Summer of 1919 by Nalty and by Lewis[4] was a prelude to that period of patriotic xenophobia in the United States sometimes called the Red Scare. A summary description of the salient features of those times in which the color red was so commonly used, and some of its antecedents, is provided by Johnson. Features of the period are the ferment over unrestricted immigration, the so-called Bolshevik scare accompanied by mass fear of treason and sedition, infringement of individual citizenship rights by state and federal governments, an upsurge of interest in the Ku Klux Klan, increasing evidence of massive anti-Semitism, and the passage of national legislation establishing racial or ethnic immigration quotas. Johnson observes, in describing the situational context of the Jewish American community, that

> Numbering over four and a half million by 1925 it was in the rapid process of becoming the largest, richest and most influential Jewish community in the world. Judaism was America's third religion. The Jews were not merely accepted, they were becoming part of the American core and already making decisive contributions to shaping the American matrix. They never had the financial leverage which, from time to time, they secured in some European countries, because by the 1920s the American economy was so enormous that no one group, however large, could become dominant in it. But in banking, stockbroking, real estate, retail, distribution and entertainment, the Jews occupied positions of strength. More important, perhaps, was the growing Jewish success in the professions, made possible by the enthusiasm with which Jewish families seized on the opportunities open to them in America to secure a higher education for their children. Some colleges, especially in the Ivy League, ran Jewish quota limitation. But in practice there were no numerical restraints on the expansion of Jewish higher education.[5]

It is curious, however, to find little evidence of concerted actions between the African and Jewish American communities during this period of the Red Scare. This is the more remarkable because the founding of the major civil rights organizations — and especially those identified with the African American community — during the first decades of the twentieth century appeared to initiate a phase of close cooperation between the leadership cadres of the two minority communities. Furthermore, the bonding of the African and Jewish American alliance is said initially to have occurred between 1915 and 1923 and then to have disintegrated or temporarily collapsed in 1936.[6]

The issue becomes how to explain what seems to be a failure of alleged allies to ally interactively — that is, to negotiate, bargain, cooperate, and even conflict — during the unique experiences of the Red Scare. This is important precisely because one of the allies, the Jewish American community, if not exactly embattled, was yet the major target of a stream of generalized hatred. This evidence of environmental stress, largely from the culturally dominant European-derived Anglo-Saxon Protestant segments of American society, could not be coped with directly and aggressively; and it was generally perceived as threatening the ambiguous identity and status of the Jewish American community. The situation was ripe for that collective group response that earlier I called "defensive structuring,"[7] one version of such a response being, reasonably, the solidifying of a potential coalition or alliance with other minority groups. Such a beginning apparently had been made with the African American community.

Ample evidence establishes conclusively that by the time of the Red Scare the tradition of "being of use" to the African American community was well ingrained in the Jewish American community.[8] Grounded in the apparent strategy of establishing a presence at the center of the struggle for equality and justice of the African American community — involving intelligence, money, and influence — the Jewish American community by being of use would be able to fight anti-Semitism "undercover" or by remote control. The major vehicles designed to drive this strategy, apparently, were those of philanthropy and a highly individualized pattern of intense personal mentorship.

Some consequences of the application of this strategy of being of use to the African American community by the Jewish American community were to be observed plainly in selected realms of American life.[9] Most conspicuous are those consequences seen in such slices of American life as the distinct prominence of the Jewish American community in founding, financing, and supporting civil rights organizations in the African American community; its assisting and supporting efforts to ease the almost unprecedented urbanization problems of the African American community — involving especially pathologies of the family, women and children, work and employment, health, and housing; its sustaining and supporting the connections of the African American community to the entire apparatus of schooling in the United States, but especially so in the infamous segregated educational system of the southern region; its actively abetting the entry of African Americans into the realm of arts, letters, and aesthetic activities; and its providing guidance, advisement, and encouragement for the active participation of the African American community — not insignificantly through an introduction into Socialist and Communist politics — in local and national political arenas.[10]

At least two distinguishing features of this being-of-use strategy that was followed by the Jewish American community during the Red Scare deserves mention. First, I have been able to find no evidence establishing conclusively that the African American community was involved interactively at any time with the Jewish American community in reaching this strategy policy. There is, in other words, no accessible record or body of information describing any pertinent exchanges or transactions in reaching what must be considered a watershed policy of alliance or coalition between these two minority communities. One can only conclude, reasonably, that the policy was evolved unilaterally by the Jewish American community as part and parcel of its defensive structuring.

The second salient feature of this being-of-use strategy concerns the matter of status parity of the alleged allies — the Jewish and African American communities. That is, little evidence is available of instances in which the African American community reciprocated by being of use in those activities which were held to be of supreme importance for the unique interests of the Jewish American community. One might look in vain, for instance, for a listing similar to the one above to describe consequences of a being-of-use strategic policy affecting the Jewish American community generated by influences emerging from the African American community.

One is left, then, with the inference that from the origin and implementation of this adduced strategic policy of being of use linking the Jewish and African American communities the two parties of the alliance clearly were of unequal status — economically, politically, and culturally. Diner observes, for instance, that "The Jewish-black alliance had emerged from the almost total weakness of one party."[11] Stated more starkly, it is not unreasonable to suspect that, between these two minority communities, some elements of dependency, if not those of exploitation, strongly characterized the early or initial collaboration of the African and Jewish American communities.[12] This pattern of relationship between any special interest groups holds signal implications, of course, for issues of relative group power, control, and domination within the formation of a coalition or an alliance.

Some support for this observation about the lack of status parity in the emerging alliance at this particular time between the African and Jewish American communities is provided by taking a quick glance at their participation in the so-called radical politics of the Socialist and Communist parties during the 1920s. From the mid-nineteenth century onward into the 1920s the so-called "Negro Question," according to Foster,[13] permeated the historical evolution in the United States of what has been called the leftist political movement — the International Workingmen's Association, Marxism, the Socialist Labor Party, the Socialist Party, the American Communist Party, and the American Negro Labor Congress. The political dimensions of the so-called Negro Question were defined openly in a 1928 resolution that described the African Americans in the southern region as an oppressed nation, entitled to the right of self-determination.[14]

The paramountcy of the issues of either race or class in perceiving and resolving the situation of the African American community in the United States is, essentially, what has always been understood to be the substance of what was then called the Negro Question. In other words, management of the tormenting question of how to explain and understand the situation of the African American in American democracy seems to have been a central or driving force in the evolutionary development of most leftist or radical political movements in the United States.

In a critically significant biographical essay Cruse presents a historical description of Jewish and African American relations in the American Communist Party during the decades of the 1920s and 1930s. He concluded:

> The party experience brought out the bare realities of Negro-Jewish relations in sharp relief. The Communist party's faulty and unrealistic handling of Negro affairs placed the Jewish Communist in a strategic position to manipulate Negro affairs in a fashion that the Negro would never be allowed to do in Jewish affairs (or in the affairs of any other national group).[15]

In an earlier work, Cruse sums up African and Jewish American relations and their consequences in the leftist and radical political movement during the 1920s:

> In Negro-Jewish relations in the Communist Left there has been an intense undercurrent of jealousy, enmity and competition over the prizes of group political power and intellectual prestige. In this struggle, the Jewish intellectuals — because of superior organization, drive, intellectual discipline,

money and the motive power of their cultural compulsives — have been able to win out. In the name of Negro-white unity (the Party's main interracial slogan), the Jewish Communists acted out the role of political surrogates for the "white" working class, and thereby gained the political whip of intellectual and theoretical domination of the Negro question.[16]

If the 1920s is seen as a period in which the emerging alliance between the African and Jewish American communities began seriously to solidify, then, also, there became noticeable portentous qualities or characteristics of the alliance. Whether bound up or not with the complex ferment of the Red Scare period in America, these features of the interrelationship of the two minority communities include: a curious lack of evidence of genuine joint action; an unusual degree of environmental stress directed toward the Jewish American community and thereby tilting it toward the urgent need of searching for suitable allies; and the emergence from the Jewish American community of a policy of being of use to the African American community, which tended to link the two communities in an alliance of inequality (in terms of group dominance, control, and power).

This look at African and Jewish American community relations during the 1920s would be misleading if mention is not made of one of the most infamous anti-Semitic campaigns of the time, which was, also, intricately bound up with the Red Scare. From approximately 1920 until 1927 Henry Ford, a wealthy and prominent automobile industrialist of the state of Michigan, conducted through the press and the then new technological medium of the radio a deliberate and deadly assault upon the Jewish American community.[17] While this attack was only one aspect of a worldwide period of anti-Semitic bigotry, the American Jewish community, defending itself legally or responding largely by resort to the courts, was able by 1927 to compel Ford to publicly retract his statements and apologize.[18]

The substance of the Ford anti-Semitic campaign rested largely upon the myth of the *Protocols of the Elders of Zion,*[19] a weapon of terror perfected and used recurrently against Jewish communities in Eastern, Central, and Western Europe throughout most of the nineteenth century. This campaign of anti-Semitism contributed largely to the defensive structuring of the Jewish American community during the decade, one aspect of which was their readiness to ally with the African American community. Remarkably, throughout the entire course of the Ford anti-Semitic campaign little evidence is found of attempts by the African American community to aid, assist, or support their emergent ally.

During the latter half of the 1920s there clearly is evidence, as will be seen shortly in an examination of the advent of the Communist Party, of rapprochement between the African and Jewish American communities. The attractiveness of this coalition from the Jewish American community perspective is compounded jointly out of their defensive structuring in response to a vicious anti-Semitic campaign and the opportunity to link in a position of dominance with a weaker ally. These conditions of deepening societal hatred and discovered functional utility to an ally, moreover, contributed heavily to the transformation of the Jewish American community from an immigrant to what earlier has been referred to as middleman minority group status in American society.[20] For the African American community, during the 1920s, there was little choice given the desperation and precariousness of its societal situation. This is the only reasonable answer to the question beginning this section as to why there seem to be no clear attempts by the African American community to aid their emergent ally — the Jewish American community — during the period of the Red Scare and the nationwide campaign of anti-Semitism.

LEADERSHIP AND THE HARLEM RENAISSANCE

The African American community desperately attempted to survive and to fend off collective disillusionment during the 1920s. The definition of its collective societal situation tended to oscillate, almost eccentrically, between hope and hopelessness.

Was full Americanization possible for those who made up the African American community? A matrix of unfulfilled group expectations about equity, freedom, and justice seemed to permeate its immediate as well as its future social reality. Ultimately this reality of unfulfilled expectations was grounded in cruel problems generated simultaneously from contradictions inherent in American democracy about the stigma of inferior minority group status in an emergent liberal pluralistic state.

These cruel problems were the immediacy of the indignities of prejudicial perception and the repressions of segregative and discriminatory behaviors as practiced in a traditional "jim crow" system of dehumanization, exploitation, and oppression, and the strains and tensions of precariousness internalized within the ideology and organizational structure of the minority community. Any understanding of the process of building a coalition with the Jewish American community must come out of the fundamental dilemma inherent in this existential reality confronting the African American community. This dilemma, and especially for its individual and organized leadership elements, involved both the choice of particular goals and the selection of strategies or means suitable for their attainment by the minority community.

During those halcyon days of speakeasies, free love, and jazz — and coinciding with the flourishing of lynching — defining goals for the African American community provoked recurring crises among that leadership offered by individuals and between those public positions taken by officials representing that vast array of voluntary associations making up its organizational structure. By voluntary associations I mean the panoply of entities making up the organizational fabric of the African American community such as churches, labor unions, literary and debating societies, political and civic clubs, benevolent and fraternal organizations, such mass organizations as the NAACP, the National Urban League, and, as well, the minority community press.

The issue over which these persistent crises of goal orientation arose, within the leadership cadres of the African American community, is subject to gross oversimplification. Shortly put, it involved always tension between the extreme ideologies: that of cultural assimilation or the virtual abandonment of group identity and that of some version of nationalism stressing usually Pan-Africanism, separate development, entrepreneurship, and self-help. Essentially, however, the problem of collective goal determination evolved always into the question of whether at this particular time the African American community, as a minority group, should or should not strive for undiminished American citizenship.

The intractability of this issue of minority group end or goal for the African American community is notorious. A dimension of this intractability is described vividly by St. Clair Drake in his tracing of the "vindicationist tradition" — that stream of scholarship using a so-called Black Perspective to change both WASP [White Anglo-Saxon Protestant] and other European American attitudes and behaviors and to foster African American consciousness and solidarity.[21] In addition to the perceived recalcitrancy of the dominant European American majority toward racial equality and justice, at least two conditions directly contributed to this situation of paradox. First, there was the clashing values and goals of the emerging elements making up the increasingly diverse body of the African American community. Lewis[22] argues that the African American elite, largely composed of intellectuals, artists, entertainers, social workers, and educators located in prominent leadership positions with the National Urban League and the NAACP, tilted — with considerable reservation and hesitation — toward acceptance of the goal of assimilation. The controversy, ambiguity, and ambivalence underlying this reservation toward the goal of assimilation by the African American elite is demonstrated clearly by the convening in 1925, and the apparent failure, of the so-called Negro Sanhedrin.[23]

Opposing this irresolutely held assimilationist position of the African American leadership elite — and especially between approximately 1919 and 1925 — emerged that mass movement led by Marcus Garvey, the Universal Negro Improvement Association, advocating provocatively a doctrine of racial and cultural nationalism.[24] And, finally, there was that residue of the Booker T. Washington leadership tradition[25] that advocated for the African American community a type of benign accommodation to the prevailing racist system featuring avoidance of striving for full social and civil equality while emphasizing a kind of minority group hegemony in agriculture and the trades.

The second condition contributing to this paradox facing the emerging leadership of the African American community was the prevailing, even overwhelming, influence of the ideals, values, and objectives of both the Jewish American community and the dominant WASP community. The substance as well as the subtleties of this entanglement in the leadership process during the 1920s has been documented substantially.[26] Several consequences of this particular condition seem important in these early stages of the developing process toward some form of alliance between the African and Jewish American communities.

First, the legitimation of secular leadership, in particular, in the African American community generally tended to be tenuous. This involves, obviously, the question of *who* were the leaders, *how* was their leadership obtained, and *what* were their agendas. At the heart of the matter, ultimately, lies the issues of authority and power. Second, a definite tendency toward cleavage between the African American elite and the African American masses became more visible. This tendency was exacerbated severely by those historical strains, tensions, and conflicts apparent at least since the era of that "peculiar institution" (field versus house slaves) in the organizational evolution of the African American community and by the specific policy intent of the developing American Communist Party. Vacillation, uncertainty, and dependency, or lack of minority group hegemony within the pluralist reality of American society, thus combined to make more difficult the task of African American leadership in resolving this dilemma of community goals or ends.

Nevertheless, in spite of the intransigence of the contradictions between the ideals of human equality and the philosophical notion of liberalism and liberty that inhibited, in part, the establishment of clear minority group goals, at least two strategies clearly were adopted during the 1920s by the emerging leadership cadre of the African American community. The first was that of continued advocacy of elemental civil rights before the courts and in Congress. This strategy has, with its tactical commitment to litigation and publicity, a long record in the history of the African American community. The intent of this strategy essentially was to provide the rationale for a moral and constitutional protest against indignities imposed upon American citizens of African descent.

This strategy of litigative advocacy, apparently tested initially in early civil rights efforts between 1887 and 1908 of the Afro-American Council or the National Afro-American League,[27] was adopted by the NAACP during 1915–1916 in that organization's first successful protest action on the national level.[28] This campaign was directed against the adoption by the U.S. Congress of H.R.6060 that included an "African Exclusion Amendment" barring entry into the nation of all persons of African descent. Allegedly designed to prevent the immigration into the United States of those of African descent from the Caribbean and Latin America, as well as Africa, the defeat of this bill, according to Cruse, allegedly exerted considerable influence upon the composition and character of the African American community. It permitted, ironically, the entry into the United States of Marcus Garvey, who became a resolute opponent of the NAACP.[29]

It is well to note here three fatal weaknesses of this strategy of litigative advocacy. First, it assumed the impossible, that is, the objectivity and impartiality of the American judicial system. Second, it is alleged that "Court victories afforded [African American] leadership with maximal publicity with minimal potential to overturn the real world of race relations. . . . Given the shabby record of evasion and nonenforcement of court decisions on the state and local levels, civil rights advocates could claim important victories, and civil rights opponents could ignore them."[30] Thus, an important consequence of this strategic weakness of not achieving direct relief and results was the insidious but essential entanglement of the leadership elite cadre with WASP and Jewish American leadership elite cadres. While this entanglement sustained the litigative advocacy strategy, at least by the largess of philanthropy and the indulgences of interracial socializing, it led reasonably to suspicions of the cooptation and domination of African American leadership. In addition, it contributed to the intensification of discord, or lessening of solidarity, among the varieties of regional, national origin, religious, and social class diversities of the African American community.

The third fatal weakness of the litigative advocacy strategy was its deemphasis, or apparent disregard, of the political economy aspects of the contextual situation in which the African American community was embedded within American society. This matter of the relative priority of economic and political rights versus the values of noneconomic liberalism and legal redress is an ancient and endemic issue within the ideological ferment of the civil rights struggle of the African American community.[31] Stemming at least from the controversies during the late nineteenth and early twentieth centuries surrounding the posture of Booker T. Washington, this issue allegedly led, ultimately, to the tacit severance during the 1930s of official relations of DuBois and other prominent leaders with the NAACP and the National Urban League. Also, according to Cruse, "It was precisely over the issue of *economics* (Jewish versus black economics) that the black-Jewish alliance collapsed in 1935 and entered a stage of disintegration leading to the 1960 era with its rise in vocal black anti-Semitism."[32]

The second strategy adopted ingeniously by the rising leadership cadre of the African American community was infiltration of the aesthetic domain of American culture. The domain of the arts, letters, and culture, in other words, was to be used instrumentally as a weapon of the civil rights movement. This was the essence of that period of creative brilliance by African Americans during the 1920s commonly known as the Harlem Renaissance.[33]

Two notions provided the foundation for what was essentially the nonaesthetical or political meaning of the Harlem Renaissance for the African American community. There was, first, the premise that the most powerful and significant factor for changing the repression and exclusion of the African American community at this particular time was interracial contacts and friendships, especially for those who were educated, privileged or socially acceptable, and talented. With this notion was yoked the insight that in all American culture there was only one nonproscribed area for African Americans — the aesthetic. In other words, African American creativity and expressiveness were to be used in the civil rights struggle for equality and justice as *a negotiable power of exchange — a commodity for bargaining.*[34]

Two key networks of leaders — all located in the North but exerting nationwide influence — have been identified as implementing these two basic strategies of the African American community. The first may be called a political action network composed primarily of Fred R. Moore, editor and publisher of *The New York Age*; T. Thomas Fortune, former editor of *The Age,* then editor of the Garvey publications; Ferdinand G.

Morton, leading Harlem Democrat and head of that special "Negro" organization of the local Democratic Party, established earlier by Edward E. Lee and called the United Colored Democracy; Edward A. Johnson, Harlem's first Assemblyman; and the militant African American socialist, nationalist and Garveyite, Hubert H. Harrison.[35]

The second network of leaders may be identified as cultural or literary. Its primary actors were Charles S. Johnson, sociologist and educator; Jessie Redmon Fauset, writer and editor; Alain Leroy Locke, philosopher and educator; Walter White, NAACP executive; Casper Holstein, reputed policy banker and philanthropist; and James Weldon Johnson, a renaissance man. Without these exemplars of superb commitment to the fate of African Americans, according to Lewis,[36] the Harlem Renaissance roster of twenty-six novels, ten volumes of poetry, five Broadway plays, innumerable essays and short stories, two or three performed ballets and concerti, and the large output of canvas and sculpture would have been a great deal shorter and less impressive.

These leadership networks established and maintained extensive linkages throughout the African American community nationally — and even those remnants of it scattered internationally — while located and operating largely out of Harlem. A variety of devices became the tools used by these network linkages. As highly articulate advisors on the civil rights struggle to, and even social intimates with, many philanthropists of the Jewish American and WASP communities and with politicians and other public officials, the members of these two networks became, essentially, highly dedicated and astute brokers for almost all phases of the complex civil rights movement. Contacts were maintained with the fading Booker T. Washington machine in Tuskegee, Alabama, the UNIA of Marcus Garvey, and W. E. B. DuBois, who resided then in Harlem. Contact was maintained as well with leadership subcenters of the African American community active throughout the nation, especially in Philadelphia, Washington, D.C., Atlanta, Nashville, and Chicago. Almost all aspects of African American life during these times were touched — indirectly if not directly — by the efforts of these political action and cultural/literary networks of the African American community.

The close interlocking of the cultural/literary and political action networks must be assumed, but in at least one respect they were as one. They had the paramount task, in masterminding the civil rights struggle of the African American community, of assembling, managing, and attempting to manipulate Jewish American and WASP patrons with the bargaining chips of potential electoral power; cultural creativity and expressiveness; and serviceability as a displaced or substitute object for anti-Semitism or bigotry. At the same time they had to tend the continuing legitimation of their leadership hegemony within the African American community.

It is most significant, too, that at this time a certain awareness, emerging within these two leadership cadres of the African American community but with historical antecedents, became a definite conscious-ness. This consciousness expansion involved the perception of the worldwide universality of the dilemma of those of African descent in the African Diaspora, that is, in the Middle East, Western Europe, Canada, the Caribbean, Central and South America, and the United States. This consciousness, as well as its political implications, was nurtured by additions to the African American community of immigrants from other communities of the African Diaspora,[37] the mass movement of Marcus Garvey, participation in socialistic and eventually communistic activities, and varied contacts established in connection with the birth of the League of Nations and other post–World War I arrangements.

Thus, as the need for a coalition became more urgent between the Jewish and African American communities and the dynamics of the process became more intense, fallouts from the fundamental contradic-tions between the strategies of political economy versus litigative advocacy as well as the politics of aestheticism had to be struggled with by the African American leadership cadre.

An affinity for mugwumg or clientage politics — as described in Chapter 2 — as well as almost utter dependency upon Jewish and WASP patronage (with the accompanying risks of charges of cooptation and domination) and that tendency toward heavy reliance for redress and relief upon federal rather than state or local governmental agencies all became distinguishing features of leadership style in the African American community. These minority group leadership characteristics, when confronted with the being-of-use strategy of the Jewish American community, were of incalculable significance in implanting a quality of almost utter dependency upon the role of the African American community within that coalition process then under way between the two minority communities.

THE GREAT DEPRESSION AND THE NEW DEAL

Those early efforts of negotiating, bargaining, and cooperating — and their exploratory testing for suitability as part of a special relationship or coalition — that were begun during the first three decades of the century to merge the interests of the African and Jewish American communities, were powerfully enhanced in the 1930s by the massive social forces and devastating conditions then pervading the world. Within this cauldron of social change in the United States the fundamental aims of the Jewish American community were to minimize the potential of those particular forces in America suspected of being linked to anti-Semitism and to nurture those particular forces seemingly conducive to maintaining collective identity and solidarity. One of the means chosen to accomplish these aims was the establishment by ideology, intelligence, money, and influence of domination over that ubiquitous movement for civil rights found throughout the African American community.[38]

The overreaching aim of the African American community, at the same time, was to forge the conditions for compensation for the inequities of group ascendancy as well as status discrepancy. In short, the aim was justice and equity within America for the African American community. This general aim, agreed on as reasonable policy largely during the preceding decade, was to be achieved by both engaging in the politics of the arts, or bartering creativity and expressiveness as a negotiable power of exchange, and continuing the strategy of legitimation of the philosophy of noneconomic liberalism that was begun during previous decades.[39]

Massive, even radical, transformation of the religious, economic, political, and cultural institutions of the nation was occurring during the decade of the 1930s.[40] Concrete implications of this reformation for the developing alliance and coalition between the Jewish and African American communities are almost impossible to discern. While a profile of some of these societal forces, conditions, and events may suggest the futility of performing such a task, it may point also to the relevancy of such existential conditions for understanding the predicament of these two minority communities.

There was, to begin, the failure of that ubiquitous alliance between business and politics culminating in the economic crisis of 1929 and the subsequent disenchantment with those elites then controlling the government and the nation. Foster, in describing the depression which followed the crash of the stock market, noted that "Millions of workers must go hungry because there is too much wheat. Millions of workers must go without clothes because the warehouses are full to overflowing with everything that is needed. Millions of workers must freeze because there is too much coal. This is the logic of the capitalist system."[41]

The passage of the Hawley-Smoot Tariff Act, which badly disrupted trade relations with other nations of the world, was followed, inevitably, by a worldwide financial crisis. And a series of bank runs, failures, and holidays eliminated confidence in the fiscal institutions of the United States. Major regions of the country were subjected to natural devastation such as droughts and floods disrupting agriculture and other extractive industries and major sectors of the national economy.

Incidents of racial hatred, violence, calculated repression, and miscarriages of justice were legend. The instance of the Scottsboro Cases and the saga of Angelo Herndon are representative of the decade. In 1935 a bitter riot, which took place in Harlem, was notable for its alleged anti-Semitic manifestations.

A development that cannot be overlooked was the emergence into prominence of the Communist Party.[42] Its visible influence permeated circles of power that included intelligentsia, academe and education, organized labor, the mass media, entertainment, the arts, and the federal government. From about 1928 to the onset of World War II, in fact, no organization or mass movement seems to have exerted as significant an impact upon the consciousness and the social structure of the African American community — and the process of alliance or coalition formation between the African and Jewish American communities — as did the Communist Party.[43]

I am amazed at the lack of recognition given by analysts of the African American protest and struggle for racial equality in America to the contributions of Communist Party members such as Otto Huiswoud, Cyril Briggs, Richard Moore, Grace Campbell, Lovett Fort-Williams, James Ford, Benjamin Davis, Jr., Theodore Bassett, Abner Berry, Bonita Williams, Merrill Work, Rose Gaulden, Claudia Jones, Audley Moore, and Howard Johnson.[44] While Communist Party affairs apparently were centered in and managed mainly out of New York City, as a catalyst for change in the African American community its influence was felt nationwide. It merits special notice that this influence of the Communist Party on the African American community was felt in the larger cities of the far west and the Midwest and, surprisingly, in the rural as well as the urban areas of the South.

The ultimate goal, at this time, of the Communist Party to capture or revolutionize the African American community failed. However, its campaign became a substantial part of the entire process of self-identification, consciousness raising, and collective solidarity being created by this minority community. The Communist Party, by its policies and practices, helped tilt the goal orientation of the African American community away from that of separatism and racial nationalism toward the goal of integration. Its assault complicated the diversity and heterogeneity of the leadership and the organizational character of the

African American community by courting and attacking, simultaneously, its intellectual cadre, its middle class, and its churches.

The Communist Party challenged the, by then, institutionalized tactics of accommodative reformism, litigative advocacy, and paternalism largely employed in the African American community by offering novel alternatives. These major alternatives were systematic community organizing and direct confrontational actions such as rallies, boycotts, demonstrations, and mass protests. Also, they committed that horror (according to some) of publicly exposing, relentlessly and painstakingly, the latent or disguised cleavages and the contradictory self-interests of the intellectual cadre, the middle classes, and the working classes making up the social structure of the African American community. The Communist Party flamboyantly addressed, nationally and internationally, controversial issues that were cruelly demoralizing the African American masses, for example, lynchings and judicial injustices in the cases of the Scottsboro Boys and union organizing in the case of Angelo Herndon.

In selected places throughout the nation the Communist Party battled fiercely with the traditional leadership cadres (for example, the NAACP, the intellectuals and literati, the churches, and other mass organization functionaries) for control of the working classes of the African American community by advocating vociferously for new approaches to resolving such issues as tenants' rights, organized labor's rejection and discrimination, the availability and quality of schooling, problems of unemployment, police brutality, disenfranchisement, discrimination in employment, denials of civil rights and civil liberties, and, in the urban areas of the North, the lack of forceful participation in electoral politics. In fact, it would seem that the Communist Party experienced some success in inclining the traditional leadership cadres of the African American community toward using lobbying and legislative action as a major part of active participation in the political process.

Several aspects of Communist Party policy and practice, throughout the vast reaches of the African American community, appear to have contributed directly toward building the nascent alliance between the African and Jewish American communities. First, Jewish Americans seem to have made up a sizeable component of the then highly ethnically stratified divisions of the Communist Party; and they were assigned by policy to recruitment and program work in the African American community, North and South. A striking representation of the Jewish American community, therefore, was actively involved in dealing on a daily, face-to-face basis with African Americans, thereby enhancing a novel kind of interracial contact.[45]

The effects of these contacts were especially noteworthy, as they were driven by the principle of interracialism and were, therefore, new experiences for most members of the African American community. For the Communist Party advocated and practiced insistently the complete racial integration of all (social, political, and cultural) aspects of Party life. These Jewish American true believers of the Communist Party (although sometimes condemned for arrogance and insensitivity) bore witness to the egalitarian values of human dignity, racial equality, and individual freedom, and this lesson was not lost on the African American community.

Second, the Communist Party joined the African American community in defining positively, rather than rejecting, its cultural and artistic contributions and potentials for the nation. Thus, the Communist Party and the African American community together placed the unique creativities of the latter in the realms of music, art, dance, theatre, language, and sense of style squarely within the struggle for racial equality and justice; and, in fact, the Communist Party led in redefining this aspect of the African American experience as a source of cultural regeneration for the entire nation. It must be noted, too, that within the ideological clamor of the African American community the Communist Party touched off, deliberately, an intense debate over the relative importance of the values of instruction or entertainment in those aesthetical spheres of sports, music, painting and sculpting, theatre and drama, and literature.[46]

Third, the emphasis placed by the Communist Party upon electoral politics helped lead the African American community closer to the strategies and tactics then being used so successfully by the Jewish American community. This changed emphasis thereby provided another area of partnership and coalition between the two minority communities. Eventually, this emphasis upon electoral politics was subtly shifted from disruption and mass demonstrations to lobbying and legislative actions which, again, provided an opportunity for allies to bargain, negotiate, cooperate, and conflict.

And, fourth, the policies and actions of the Communist Party in the arenas of the organized labor movement, the "leftist" intellectual community, and, as opponents of war and fascism were determinative in influencing the rapprochement toward alliance of the African and Jewish American communities. This development could only have contributed to the broadening of the perspective of the African American community to international developments. It thereby coincided with the increased concern of the Jewish American community for the worldwide perils of Nazism and the accelerated anti-Semitism then being felt in the United States. Finally, the open espousal of a "Negro-Jewish alliance" by the Communist Party at this time contributed without any doubt to the nascent coalition of these two minority communities.[47]

In short, then, the precise matrix of factors contributing to this crystallization of the alliance or coalition between the African and Jewish American communities and the Communist Party can only be surmised. Yet, the nature of the work of the Communist Party during the Great Depression is conjectured by Smith as being a crucial ingredient.[48] He suggests that the matrix of factors would include such working principles — exercised in both the North and the South — as selfless work by individual Party members and fellow travelers in the immediate causes of the poor and oppressed; the glorification of "the worker"; organizers of unions for the labor movement; intractable espousal of the human rights of African Americans; leadership of those people's organizations called the "Unemployed Councils"; and opposition to fascism and other forms of oppression and repression.

Nevertheless, two developments during this period between the two world wars adversely affected the process of alliance between these two minority communities. These developments were the Harlem race riot in the spring of 1935, with its open charges of African American anti-Semitism,[49] and the threatening meanings given to the rise of fascism and the accompanying nationalistic feelings among the Jewish American community at the advent of Nazism in Europe.[50] The legacy of these two developments was explicit tensions between the allied minority communities that were to continue sporadically until the present time. Thus, the viability of the alliance would hereafter be subject to considerable strain, if not occasionally disintegration, by the different burdens of history borne by the two minority groups and by the selective meanings or interpretations given to specific situational crises of the African and Jewish American communities.

Along with the prominent role of the Communist Party, as described above, in the process of coalition formation between the African and Jewish American communities, other curious forces with possible implications for this coalition process were making their presences felt in the nation. The specter of fascism surfaced in the United States while it emerged as Nazism in Germany, and other variants of totalitarianism appeared in Italy, Spain, and Japan. Emerging also was itinerant evangelism under the leadership of Dwight Moody, Gipsy Smith, Billy Sunday, Aimee Semple McPherson, and Cyclone Mack. Other radical mass movements such as the Bonus Expeditionary Armies, Father

Devine's Peace Missions, and others such as Elder Micheaux, Lucy Smith, and Rose Horn mobilized throughout the land.[51] President Hoover's rough military control of one such insurgent movement — the Bonus Expeditionary Army — resulted later in the prominent careers of subsequent military leaders such as MacArthur, Eisenhower, and Patton while increasing the demoralization of the nation.

An answer for the nation, dangerously demoralized by the Depression, arose in the birth of the New Deal with President Franklin D. Roosevelt and the transfer of prevailing control of the federal government in 1932 from the Republican to the Democratic Party. Out of this transfer of legitimacy and power within the nation came the design and implementation of the labor- and capital-intensive alphabet programs of relief (Works Progress Administration and Public Works Administration, respectively) by largely a new breed of federal bureaucrats.

Again, as in the instance of the Communist Party, representatives of the Jewish American community were prominent in this new breed of federal bureaucrats.[52] Considerable emphasis was placed upon patronage of the arts by programs of the New Deal, and special attempts seem to have been made to utilize members of the African American community. Concluding this overview of the 1930s are the fascist military aggression of Italy against Ethiopia in 1935,[53] the infamous treason trials of the Soviet Union, the saga of the International Brigade during the Spanish Civil War, and the immigrant wave to the United States of Jewish intellectuals escaping from Nazi Germany and Austria — all heralding the onset of World War II.

Out of the above cauldron of social change the process of alliance — negotiatng, bargaining, cooperating, and conflicting — between the African and Jewish American communities during the 1930s tended to cluster about three interlocking issues. First, within both minority communities a continual debate took place between the politics of nationalism and those of assimilation. It would be a gross oversimplification of the issue, however, to assume that it had the same meaning for both communities. On one hand, the Jewish American community, tilting toward assimilation or nationalism, was complicated by such factors as collective fears of incipient anti-Semitism in the United States, the rise of Nazism in Germany, the growing legitimation of the Zionist movement, and the emerging prominence of Jewish Americans in local, state, and federal political arenas. Also, within the Jewish American community, the proponents of assimilation, cultural pluralism, and Zionism — aligned essentially along the axes of social class and Eastern or Western

European origin — intensified their ideological disputes during these times of the Depression and the New Deal.

On the other hand, within the African American community there was increased disillusionment with the approach of noneconomic liberalism as a method of social change in the civil rights movement. Marable comments that

> Du Bois recognized the trend towards accommodation within the NAACP and the Negro elite generally, and attempted to combat it during the Great Depression. In an April 1933 essay in the NAACP journal, *Crisis,* he urged the Black middle class to recognize the limits of bourgeois liberalism and clientage with the major parties. "We must have power; we must learn the secret of economic organization," he argues.[54]

The growing consensus between African and Jewish American elites represented by the strategies of being of use and of the politics of the arts (the use of creativity and expressiveness as a negotiable power of exchange), along with their mutual entanglement in the Communist Party, grew out of the ramification of dealing with this perennial issue of accommodation or reform. Lewis concludes that not until the mid-1930s did African American leaders "begin to appreciate some of the limitations of litigation and literature and the potential of alliance with the liberal wing of the Democratic party and of the more racially progressive labor unions."[55]

However, growing accommodative consensus between the elites of the Jewish and African American communities did not necessarily hold for all parts of these minority communities. Thus, the second interlocking issue around which negotiation, bargaining, and cooperation toward alliance and coalition tended to converge was the applicability of a class or a race approach to understanding and resolving the racial situation in the United States.

While debate, since at least the 1890s, about the relative importance of the factors of race and class in the deadly serious game of racial politics has always been intense, during the 1930s it surfaced with a vengeance. Lewis observes that, as a consequence or legacy of the Garvey movement, "For the first time outside the genteel sphere of literature, the concealed tensions and subconscious antipathies of dark and light Afro-Americans were furiously exposed and nurtured."[56] Essentially, Marcus Garvey politicized the color taboos of the African American community by bringing out into the open the correspondence between social position and skin color, and this reality was very disturbing to the leadership cadre of the minority group.

The leadership of the Garvey movement, it is important to note here, was mainly of West Indian origin; and the rejection of the legitimacy claims of the traditional leadership of the African American community as well as the advocacy of a kind of cultural nationalism was a troublesome issue that contributed to a significant cleavage within the minority community. It was especially troublesome since the Garvey movement had some appeal not only to West Indians of African descent but also to the African American masses. In another cogent comment about this controversy of race and class, Lewis observes "that on those few occasions in the early 1930s when the Talented Tenth mobilized the masses to protest economic discrimination, its specific demands were usually for middle-class advancement."[57]

Marable catches another facet of the confounding of this issue of race and class in the mobilization of the African American community. According to him, "Most Black elected officials at any one time belong to the same party (Republican, pre-1940; Democrat, post-1940); they are recruited from the Afro-American petty [sic] Bourgeoisie — lawyers, doctors, ministers, entrepreneurs, teachers, landlords, administrators; they frequently use appointive and elective positions to improve their social class position and to accumulate capital."[58] The play of the factor of class, according to Lewis,[59] was prominent in the social mobility engendered by the Harlem Renaissance movement; as he argues it was a generation-skipping affair, "diverting to its ranks men and women who, in the natural course of events, would have devoted their exclusive energies to teaching, lawyering, doctoring, fixing teeth, and burying." And, from another perspective, Cruse describes in considerable detail the essence of this entanglement between race and class in the dynamics of the struggle for leadership — as well as for theoretical hegemony — within the Communist Party between African and Jewish American members.[60]

Joining with the interlocking factors of the politics of nationalism and of assimilation, and the conflict over a race or class approach to the racial situation, was the third factor of relief from the violence and repression directed incessantly, and almost solely, against the members of the African American community. During the 1930s issues of minority status involving the Jewish American community primarily concerned restrictive covenants, social acceptance, intermarriage, and quotas for admission to elite institutions of higher education. Its situation with regard to collective violence and repression — police brutality, lynching, political disenfranchisement, segregated public facilities, segregated and inferior schooling, relegation to serving essentially as a reserve labor pool, and ridicule and dehumanization in the mass media and media of popular entertainment —

was distinctly unlike that confronting the African American community. The members of the Jewish American community did not have that experience of violation said by many observers of race relations to be central to all African Americans' experience of life and culture in the United States.[61]

As a consequence, therefore, of not being the major, and direct or open, target for civil liberties and civil rights abuse the Jewish American community strategically was free to cooperate with relatively little risk in those efforts of the African American community to secure relief. Furthermore, it was to the long range survival interests of the Jewish American community to cooperate, desiring as it did to become an integral part of American society. Yet this community tended to question the ethics and morality of a nation permitting such treatment to another minority group.

A litany of the oppression and repression of the African American community during the 1930s would include abject rural and urban poverty, lynching, miscarriages of justice, and all of the human capital consequences — psychic, economic, political, and educational — of the functioning of the then intact racist system of segregation and discrimination. In the early 1930s an event began that would be known later as the infamous syphilis experiment on African Americans in Alabama.[62] This genocidal episode involved collaboration between the Veterans Hospital at the noted Tuskegee Institute, county and state health departments, the U.S. Public Health Service, private nurses and physicians, at least one nationally prominent philanthropic foundation, and significant elements of the medical and scientific professional bureaucracies of the nation.

With the notorious court cases involving the Scottsboro Boys and Angelo Herndon during the 1930s the linking of mutual interests among the Communist Party, the Jewish American community, and the African American community became more visible. Conflict was intense between these several interest groups over whether or not to conduct legal defenses, under whose auspices these litigations were to be identified, and what strategies and tactics were to be employed. The essential point to be made, however, is that in spite of the disputes and disagreements surrounding this famous round of litigation, which had found national and international audiences, bargaining and cooperation between these two minority communities tended to shape them toward a working combination.

Attempts up to this time to secure a federal anti-lynch law and to promote various legal assaults upon laws requiring racial segregation in public facilities largely had been unsuccessful. The conduct of such attempts was both costly and time consuming. A change of emphasis was called for. Consequently, during the mid-1930s, a decision was made to involve the leadership of both the Jewish and African American communities in pursuing a legal strategy directed almost solely against school segregation. This decision (to be known later as the Educational Strategy of the NAACP), and its implementation by African and Jewish American attorneys,[63] was to prove to be the foundation for key decisions of the U.S. Supreme Court during the 1940s and 1950s involving public elementary and secondary schooling as well as higher education.[64]

On March 19, 1935, an event occurred that severely strained the status of the special relationship or bonding being crystallized between the Jewish and African American communities. This event was the outbreak of what came to be called the Harlem Riot.[65] For the first time, and without ambiguity, the phenomenon emerged into the public domain that came to be labelled "black anti-Semitism" by many observers. Key issues contributing to the surfacing at this time of this alleged anti-Semitism were the particularity of the predicament of the urban African American community; the distinctive contacts and interrelationships, developed between individuals of the two minority communities, emerging out of the ramifications of a peculiar entrepreneurial tradition of the Jewish American community and the exigency of the African American community;[66] and the struggle for dominance between the African and Jewish American leadership elites involving what has been called a double standard of group (moral, ethical, and racial) judgment alleged to negate the intellectual and political autonomy of the African American community.[67] This incident was to have immense immediate as well as future influence on the process of alliance — that special relationship — between the African and Jewish American communities.

Thus, during the two decades between World Wars I and II the essential attitude toward the Jewish American community in American culture may be described as benign pluralism and that toward the African American community as malign pluralism. Clearly this period was marked by a recognition by these two minority communities of their mutual interests within American society. This perception of their perilous predicament as minority groups, moreover, was converted through a subtle relational process. This process required the balancing of distinct internal as well as external existential realities of the two minority communities. The perception was converted into concrete ways of determining joint policy and organizing agencies for transforming policy into coordinated and cooperative collective actions. This relational process was largely an exploratory one that involved discovering common areas of collective concern and applying what may be called a trial-and-error approach to achieve unified action in addressing such concerns.

Sources of discord within this special relationship of the Jewish and African American communities also emerged during these decades. Worthy of note especially were clues of the looming atrocity of the Holocaust in Europe (and its definition by the American government), implications of the strengthening legitimation of the Zionist movement, the widening discrepancy between the relative social status of the two minority communities within American society, and allegedly latent anti-Semitism within, at least, the urban sector of the African American community.

Nevertheless, developmental stages of the incipient process of alliance and coalition between these two minority communities now can be discerned. The period from about 1890 to 1915 can be described as largely an invisible exploratory stage. Relations between the African and Jewish American communities were primarily on an individual basis. Selected individuals of the two minority communities bonded to discuss perceived common problems and to cooperate in the creation of selected organizations or agencies. There was considerable eccentric philanthropic activity.

The second developmental stage of the alliance or coalition formation, the initial bonding into a special relationship between the two minority communities, seems to have taken place largely between 1915 and the mid-1930s. There was cooperation on the national political level on several specific issues, the strategy of being of use was honed, philanthropic activities were increased and more finely focused, and there was close cooperation in the refined use of the politics of the arts. Some discord in the special relations between the African and Jewish American communities appeared during the mid- and late 1930s; these attendant strains and tensions contributed, in all probability, to an apparent weakening of the ties of alliance and coalition over the next ten or twelve years.

But the ideological ferment within both communities over issues such as noneconomic liberalism, the tactics to achieve justice and equity, the goal of assimilation, and the most significant presence of the Communist Party in highly visible legal cases and in support of organized labor bolstered the sense of common interests of both minority communities. A continuity was provided — and especially noteworthy was their ostensible success in tilting the federal government toward support of the civil rights movement — for other stages of the process of alliance between these two minority communities that partially spilled over into the following period of war, the dilemmas of peace, and national recovery.

NOTES

1. See Paul Johnson, *A History of the Modern World* (London: Weidenfeld and Nicolson, 1983), pp. 1–48.

2. Ibid., p. 22.

3. Ibid., p. 14.

4. Nalty, *Strength for the Fight*, pp. 125–42; and David Levering Lewis, *When Harlem Was in Vogue*, pp. 23–24. In another account of this period from an African American perspective the summer of 1919 was "called the Red Summer because of the quantity of blood spilled in race riots all through the country." Especially see pp. 178–89 of Arthur E. Barbeau and Florette Henri, *The Unknown Soldiers: Black Troops in World War I* (Philadelphia: Temple University Press, 1974).

5. Johnson, *History of the Jews*, pp. 459–60. In another reference to these times Johnson (*A History of the Modern World*, p. 206) comments:

> On New Year's Day, 1920, in a series of concerted raids, his [Palmer's] Justice Department agents rounded up more than 6,000 aliens, most of whom were expelled. In the 'Red Scare' that followed, five members of the New York State Assembly were disbarred for alleged socialism and a congressman was twice thrown out of the House of Representatives; and two Italians, Nicola Sacco and Bartolomeo Vanzetti, anarchists who had evaded military service, were convicted of murdering a Massachusetts paymaster in a highly prejudicial case which dragged on until 1927.

For other details of this time period see Baltzell, *Protestant Establishment*, p. 199. Much has been written about life during this time. The following have been especially helpful: John Dos Passos, *Nineteen* (New York: Signet, 1932); Lewis, *When Harlem Was in Vogue*; Page Smith, *Redeeming the Time: A People's History of the 1920s and The New Deal* (New York: McGraw-Hill, 1987); Foster, *The Negro People*; Myers, *History of Bigotry*; Cruse, *Plural but Equal* (New York: Morrow, 1987); and Cruse, *Crisis of the Negro Intellectual*.

6. Cruse, *Plural but Equal*, pp. 119–21, 148.

7. Siegel, *Defensive Structuring and Environmental Stress*, pp. 11–21, and "The African American Community" section of my Chapter 1.

8. See Lewis, *When Harlem Was in Vogue*, pp. 99–103.

9. See Berson, *Negroes and the Jews*, pp. 82–95; Diner, *In the Almost Promised Land*, Chapters 3 and 4; Lewis, *When Harlem Was in Vogue*, pp. 100–1; Lewis, "Parallels and Divergences," especially pp. 552–61; Foster, *The Negro People*, pp. 422–29; and Cruse, *Plural but Equal*, especially Part III.

10. A definitive treatment of the involvement of the Jewish and African American communities with communism is to be found in Smith, *Redeeming the Time*; see

especially Chapter 9, "The Left," pp. 182–210; Chapter 10, "Black Americans," pp. 211–62; and Chapter 24, "Black America and the Communist Party," pp. 575–96.

11. Diner, *In the Almost Promised Land,* p. 240.

12. A common sensing of this status inequality — possibly involving dependency, exploitation, and domination — between the alliance partners is found to permeate the works of many scholars. See especially Diner, *In the Almost Promised Land,* pp. 154 and 240; Cruse, *Plural but Equal,* pp. 123–25; Cruse, "My Jewish Problem and Theirs," in *Black Anti-Semitism and Jewish Racism,* ed. by James Baldwin, et al. (New York: Richard W. Baron, 1969), pp. 171–84; Cruse, *The Crisis of the Negro Intellectual* (New York: Morrow, 1967); Lewis, "Parallels and Divergences," pp. 543–44; Alphonso Pinkney, "Recent Unrest Between Blacks and Jews: The Claims of Anti-Semitism and Reverse Discrimination," *The Black Scholar* 8:1-4 (Fall/Spring 1978/79): 55; and Reed, *The Jesse Jackson Phenomenon,* pp. 89–98.

13. Foster, *The Negro People,* Chapters 37 and 42.

14. Ibid., p. 461.

15. Cruse, "My Jewish Problem," pp. 171, 175. See also pp. 169–70.

16. Cruse, *Crisis of the Negro Intellectual,* p. 169.

17. See especially Myers, *History of Bigotry,* Chapters XXIV and XXV. Also Berson, *The Negroes and the Jews,* pp. 50–51; Frederick Lewis Allen, *Only Yesterday* (New York: Harper & Row, 1931), pp. 52–62.

18. Myers, *History of Bigotry,* Chapters XXIV and XXV.

19. See especially Johnson, *History of the Jews,* pp. 455–59; Myers, *History of Bigotry,* Chapter XXIV.

20. Bonacich, "A Theory of Middleman Minorities"; Zenner, *Middleman Minority Theories*; and Blalock, *Toward a Theory of Minority-Group Relations,* as found in note 28 of Chapter 2.

21. St. Clair Drake, *Black Folk Here and There: An Essay in History and Anthropology* (Los Angeles: University of California Center for Afro-American Studies, 1987), pp. xviii–xxiii. Drake suggests that a "Black Perspective" means that interpretation of social "reality as perceived, conceptualized, and evaluated by individuals who are stigmatized and discriminated against because they are designated as 'Negro' or 'Black.'"

22. Lewis, "Parallels and Divergences," pp. 543–44.

23. Cruse, *Plural but Equal,* pp. 126–33. Supposedly inspired by Dean Kelly Miller of Howard University, allegedly with the assistance of Alain Locke, 300 delegates from 63 organizations were convened in Chicago during 1924 to formulate a representative national council patterned after the ancient Jewish Sanhedrin.

24. Lewis, "Parallels and Divergences," pp. 556–59; Cruse, *Plural but Equal,* pp. 127–28; Foster, *The Negro People,* Chapter 41. It is hard to overestimate the role Garveyism played in creating a nationalist consciousness — an Africanist ideology — which permeated all African American leadership, individualistic and organizational, in the 1920s. See especially Clarke, *Marcus Garvey,* Parts III and IV. See also Cronon, *Black Moses.*

25. Samuel R. Spencer, *Booker T. Washington and the Negro's Place in American Life* (Boston: Little, Brown, 1955); Emma L. Thornbrough, *Booker T. Washington* (Englewood Cliffs, NJ: Prentice-Hall, 1969); Harlan, *Booker T. Washington,* Vol. 1; Harlan, *Booker T. Washington,* Vol. 2. Also, Foster, *The Negro People,* Chapter 38.

26. Cruse, *Plural but Equal*; Cruse, "My Jewish Problem"; Cruse, *Crisis of the Negro Intellectual*; Lewis, *When Harlem Was in Vogue*; Diner, *In the Almost Promised Land*; Berson, *Negroes and the Jews*; and Reed, *Jesse Jackson Phenomenon*.

27. Cruse, *Plural but Equal*, pp. 9–11.

28. Other early national-level protests organized by the leadership of the African American community included anti-lynching bills (e.g., Dyer and Castigan-Wagner); the attempt to suppress D.W. Griffith's film *The Birth of a Nation*; the U.S. Supreme Court "mob spirit" case in Arkansas of *Moore v. Buckley*. A prime purpose of African American leadership in these early litigative and other advocacy instances was to mobilize interracial support and assistance; such assistance from the Jewish American community was especially conspicuous through most of them.

29. Cruse, *Plural but Equal*, pp. 82–83.

30. Lewis, "Parallels and Divergences," p. 559.

31. Cruse, *Plural but Equal*, pp. 123, 126; Lewis, "Parallels and Divergences," pp. 563–64; and Manning Marable, *Black American Politics: From the Washington Marches to Jesse Jackson* (London: Verso, 1985), pp. 125–90.

32. Cruse, *Plural but Equal*, p. 148.

33. There is a vast body of literature on the so-called Harlem Renaissance. For this section I rely heavily upon the works of Lewis, *When Harlem Was in Vogue*; and Lewis, "Parallels and Divergences."

34. Houston A. Baker, Jr., *Blues, Ideology and Afro-American Literature: A Vernacular Theory* (Chicago: University of Chicago Press, 1984), p. 196.

35. Clarke, *Marcus Garvey*, pp. 183–84. Care must be taken with the use of the terminology for this network of "political" action. Strong criticism has been directed by many at the leadership of the African American community during this period for its lack of emphasis on the political economy dimensions of their minority group situation within capitalistic America. Much criticism has been directed at the tendency to accept the values of noneconomic liberalism and the strategy of legal redress by African American leadership and at the same time to the tendency to disregard, or to relegate to secondary importance, the political and economic realities of minority group existence in the United States. See Cruse, *Plural but Equal*; Marable, *Black American Politics*, pp. 125–90.

36. Lewis, *When Harlem Was in Vogue*, pp. 120–21.

37. This topic deserves closer attention. An excellent but somewhat dated examination is provided by Ira De A. Reid, *The Negro Immigrant: His Background, Characteristics and Social Adjustment, 1899–1937* (New York: Columbia University Press, 1939).

38. Lewis, "Parallels and Divergences," p. 555.

39. See Cruse, *Plural but Equal*, pp. 99–176.

40. Smith, *Redeeming the Time*, especially Chapter 12, "Hoover and the Depression"; Chapter 18, "The New Deal Begins"; Chapter 23, "The Scottsboro Boys and Angelo Herndon"; Chapter 24, "Black America and the Communist Party"; Chapter 34, "Federal Project No. 1"; Chapter 35, "The South Stirs"; Chapter 36, "The New Deal"; Chapter 38, "Education"; Chapter 40, "The Popular Arts"; Chapter 43, "The Clouds of War"; and Chapter 46, "The Evaluation of Roosevelt."

41. Ibid., p. 310.

42. According to Smith, "the principal beneficiary of the financial crisis and the Depression which followed was the Communist Party" (Smith, *Redeeming the Time,* p. 310). And Smith continues, "Jews had a long tradition of concern for social justice. Eastern European Jews had a tradition of radical politics as well. They provided an important part of the leadership of the Communist Party (and all the various deviations of the left), and those for whom the Communist Party was too strong a medicine naturally gravitated to the New Deal" (p. 879).

43. An exhaustive treatment of this topic is to be found in Mark Naison, *Communists in Harlem during the Depression* (Urbana: University of Illinois Press, 1983). Also, see Smith, *Redeeming the Time,* Chapter 24; Cruse, "My Jewish Problem"; Cruse, *Crisis of the Negro Intellectual*; and Cruse, *Plural but Equal.*

44. Naison, *Communists in Harlem,* especially Part I.

45. Ibid.; see the Appendix, "Black-Jewish Relations in the Harlem Communist Party."

46. Naison, *Communists in Harlem,* pp. 140–45 and the Appendix.

47. Ibid., pp. 324–25.

48. Smith, *Redeeming the Time,* pp. 1117–22.

49. Naison, *Communists in Harlem,* pp. 203–19.

50. Ibid., especially Part 2.

51. The "Lost-Found Nation of Islam in North America," often called the "Black Muslims," under the leadership of Wallace D. Fard or F. Mohammad Ali and the Honorable Elijah Muhammad, "The Messenger," was founded in Detroit, Michigan, between 1930 and 1934. See C. Eric Lincoln, *The Black Muslims in America* (Boston: Beacon Press, 1961), pp. 10–17; and James H. Laue, "A Contemporary Revitalization Movement in American Race Relations: The 'Black Muslims,'" in James A. Geschwender, *The Black Revolt* (Englewood Cliffs, NJ: Prentice-Hall, Inc., 1971), pp. 436–48. For an excellent analysis of a unique, even radical, mass movement involved in the civil rights struggle see Robert Weisbrot, *Father Devine and the Struggle for Racial Equality* (Urbana: University of Illinois Press, 1983).

52. According to Page Smith,

> Eighty-two percent of American Jews supported Roosevelt, and Jews were prominent in his inner circle of advisers. Sam Rosenman had been one of the early members of that inner circle, a confidant and speech writer. Herbert Lehman had been a close friend and political ally in New York. The prominent Jewish financier, Henry Morgenthau, Jr., was a member of Roosevelt's Cabinet and also part of his inner circle. Felix Frankfurter was in the Roosevelt Kitchen Cabinet. Roosevelt admired Louis Brandeis and considered himself in some degree a disciple of his. Benjamin Cohen became another member of the inner circle: The New Deal was filled with brilliant young Jews, many of them proteges of Frankfurter. Roosevelt's enemies called it the "Jew Deal," and anti-Semites marked him as their enemy. . . . Jews appeared for the first time as a major influence in the highest circles of government.

Smith, *Redeeming the Time,* pp. 878–79.

53. Clarke, *Harlem: A Community in Transition,* pp. 89–93.

54. Marable, *Black American Politics,* p. 164.

55. Lewis, "Parallels and Divergences," p. 564.

56. Lewis, *When Harlem Was in Vogue*, p. 41.

57. Lewis, "Parallels and Divergences," p. 563.

58. Marable, *Black American Politics*, pp. 155–56.

59. Lewis, "Parallels and Divergences," p. 561.

60. Cruse, *Crisis of the Negro Intellectual*, pp. 147–70; and Cruse, "My Jewish Problem," pp. 171–83.

61. Leslie Catherine Sanders, *The Development of Black Theatre in America: From Shadows to Selves* (Baton Rouge: Louisiana State University Press, 1988), p. 125.

62. James H. Jones, *Bad Blood* (New York: Free Press, 1981).

63. Cruse, *Plural but Equal*, pp. 176–203.

64. The origins of this so-called educational strategy of the NAACP are obscure. However, according to one observer,

> The year of the stock market crash, 1929, the NAACP retained another Jewish lawyer, Nathan Margold, to write a blueprint for improving black rights. The book-length report argued for an attack on segregated schools and the "separate but equal" doctrine enshrined by the Supreme Court in 1896. That doctrine was the legal foundation of segregation in the South. Margold called for an attack on segregation based on the argument that black schools in the South were, in fact, woefully under-funded and inadequate. The Margold report became the bible of the NAACP's legal efforts. After the NAACP created a separate Legal Defense Fund in 1939 for tax reasons, the Margold report became its bible too.

See Jonathan Kaufman, *Broken Alliance: Turbulent Times between Blacks and Jews in America* (New York: Charles Scribner's Sons, 1988), p. 91.

65. Foster, *The Negro People*, p. 490; Cruse, *Crisis of the Negro Intellelctual*, pp. 52, 85–86; Roi Ottley, *'New World A-Coming': Inside Black America* (New York: Arno Press, 1969), pp. 122–26; Berson, *Negroes and the Jews*, p. 237; Naison, *Communists in Harlem*, pp. 140–45.

66. Berson, *Negroes and the Jews*, p. 237.

67. Cruse, "My Jewish Problem," pp. 161, 175–77.

4

Dilemmas of War and Peace: 1940–1953

Superpower status for the United States was achieved and legitimated throughout the world during the 1940s and the early part of the 1950s. The attainment of this international status was the denouement, in part, of national involvement in such events of the 1930s and the 1940s as the worldwide fiscal crisis, catastrophic natural disasters, almost universal impoverishment, near demoralization of the American citizenry, the altered role of the State in national affairs as demonstrated during the New Deal, and World War II. Thus, between approximately 1939 and 1953, the hegemony of Western European nations throughout the world was transferred effectively — indeed, almost stealthily with regard to the American public — to the United States.

The legitimation of this new international stature of the nation was obtained through the convergence of several significant fields of activity. First, the nation played a major role in the violence and terror of World War II. This was followed almost sequentially by:

the turbulence of national recovery;
the deliberate, almost single-handed, rehabilitation of the victors as well as the vanquished in World War II;
the civil rights troubles of the Truman Fair Deal;
the confronting of the "Red Menace" and the insuring of loyalty;
the development of policy and mechanism (essentially the Truman Doctrine as initiated in 1946–1947 with ringing rhetoric and brilliant orchestration and $400 million for Greece and Turkey, the Marshall Plan, and the National Atlantic Treaty Organization [NATO]) to implement the ideological obsession of helping democracy survive from the perceived peril of worldwide collectivism or communism; and
monitoring with considerable anxiety the growing unrest among nations rimming the Pacific Ocean.

During this metamorphosis of the international stature of the United States — from essentially a strategic client state of the British Empire to that of the world's policeman or the leader of the imperialistic combine protecting or advancing largely Western European interests — a continuation existed of that historical process of merging the efforts and interests of the African and Jewish American communities. By the 1930s the formation of this minority group coalition had reached the state of becoming known or implicitly recognized as a special relationship. However, larger interests, critical of the particular self-interests of both the African and Jewish American communities, surfaced during the latter half of the 1930s and solidified in the 1940s. These larger interests, somehow, seemed to slow or dampen the intensity of that continuous process of alliance between the African and Jewish American communities that had begun by at least the first decade of the century.

CRISES OF MODERN ZIONISM

From the time of the New Deal Era of the 1930s through most of the 1940s the Jewish American community augmented its collective solidarity and self-confidence so as to exert most effectively in the United States the political power created by its numbers, wealth, ideas, and ability. It was superbly organized and, within the existential context of benign pluralism it experienced, became one of the most influential minority groups in America. In fact, according to Johnson, by this time the Jewish American community had become the largest, richest, and most influential Jewish community in the world. The members of the Jewish American community were not merely accepted; they had become an integral part of the American core and were making decisive contributions conspicuously to the fundamental altering of existing institutions.[1]

The modern version of Zionism, a nationalistic liberation movement of the Jewish peoples is commonly described as one of the most divisive as well as one of the most important unifying ideologies in the social organization of the Jewish American community.[2] Berson states that "Zionism was the issue around which there formed a whole cluster of political, social and philosophic ideas about how Jews should relate to themselves and to the outside world, what their relationship to other minority groups should be and how far they should go in identifying with them."[3] And, she continues, "Jews in the United States whose major emphasis was on conforming to the American way of life did not care much about Jewish nationalism in the twenties, thirties and forties. Zionism posed a threat to their cultural if not their religious assimilation."[4]

However, while almost always being historically controversial, the paramountcy of Zionism for the Jewish American community was made complete in the early 1940s with the arrival of the first authenticated reports of the "racial hygiene" theory and policy of the Nazi regime of Germany and the subsequent resolution of these practices and policies into the malevolence of the Final Solution.[5] From the time of this fundamental crisis involving the destruction of the Jewish communities of Europe — with exceptions being very singular — all actions, all thoughts, all activities of the Jewish American community had the liberating doctrine of modern Zionism as its single point of reference. The profound effects of this legitimation of modern Zionism was to heighten both individual and collective identity and strengthen immensely the solidarity of the organized Jewish American community regardless of the individual member's place of origin, time of immigration, sectarian belief, generational status, regional location, or class.

The second crisis of the Zionist movement during the 1940s was the establishment in 1948 of the Jewish state of Israel in Palestine.[6] While considered here as separate events, it is understood that the founding of Israel and the destruction of the Jewish communities of Europe are linked organically. Thus, the Jewish American community — caught up in its legitimation of Zionism, the rapidity of its social mobility in the United States, and its resolution of the strains and tensions of the political ideologies of the left and right — became engaged throughout the nation in a period of most intensive individual and group power brokerage. During the turmoil of this brokerage a temporary period of inactivity would describe fairly the diminished nurturing of their special relationship with, and being of use to, the African American community.

In the ferment generated for the creation of Israel the Jewish American community was obliged to become involved with a wide spectrum of both domestic and international issues. Competition was intense for consensus about major issues among the nation's leaders during the 1940s. Highly visible among these competing issues were the creation of Israel, national survival needs and hegemony based on our dependency on oil from the Middle East, the access of potential allies and enemies to weaponry and technological developments, and the realignment of patterns of international trade. Thus, the Jewish American community became aggressively active in congressional lobbying, pressuring the departments of State and Defense, influencing presidential election politics, and manipulating the recently founded United Nations organization in the interest of the new state of Israel. The tactics of sponsored mass rallies, massive media advertisement, and public demonstrations in support of these several interests were widely employed within the United States by the Jewish American community.[7]

Essentially, and from the perspective of the Jewish American community, the importance of the alliance and coalition with the African American community during most of the 1940s was made secondary to that of the interests and needs of modern Zionism. Of supreme importance became unity and mobilization of the Jewish American community so as to obtain some measure of control of policy from the national centers of domestic and foreign power. Structurally, the Jewish American community had become legitimately integrated within the nation's central core, and it was in position to influence decisively the determination of priorities and to participate without constraint in the critical processes of decision making at all levels of the nation. Therefore, in dealing with the twin crises of modern Zionism the Jewish American community was a potent factor in the increased concern, as well as the growing involvement, of the nation in playing out its new role as a superpower in international affairs.

STRUGGLING FOR CIVIL RIGHTS

The general status of the African American community in the United States, in terms of justice and equity as citizens, was hardly different at the onset of World War II from that at the conclusion of World War I and during the succeeding two decades. At the beginning of World War II, the African American community's primordial quest for equality and justice had to be made secondary to the crusade for a world utopia based rhetorically upon the moral principles of the Four Freedoms — of speech and expression, of worship, from want, and from fear of other nations.[8] African Americans, as members of the most stigmatized minority group in a culture profoundly hostile to racial assimilation, were asked again to sacrifice. Essentially they were asked to demonstrate again the purity of their pain and moral superiority over other American citizens by waiting for equity and justice, yet they were expected, meanwhile, to struggle valiantly for the assorted freedoms of distant others.

As a voluntary member of the armed services during World War II I experienced, undoubtedly as did most other African American volunteers and draftees, a profound inner demoralization and individual disorientation resulting from that inescapable clash between the ideals and the reality of defending democracy, freedom, and the American way of life.[9] One result was a heightening of individual consciousness toward, even a kind of cynicism about, the promised ideal. But continued exclusion, indignities, and injustices endured by the African American community may have been also a consequence of such experiences by a sizeable and impressionable slice of the African American population. Thus, during the 1940s the minority community was caught in the cruelty of a most precarious paradox.

Within the African American community there was an apparent consensus, generally, to participate fully in all aspects of the nation's war efforts. This quest for full participation was pursued indomitably with the contingent condition that all sources and structures of racial segregation, discrimination, and prejudice were to be attacked. Tactically the manifest objective of the African American community was to continue a lesson learned during the 1930s. This lesson was to enlist the authority and power of the federal government to change or eliminate those structures and processes in the social system of the nation that maintained and perpetuated inequities and injustices based upon race.

Some gains were obtained by the African American community during the 1940s. The consciousness of the American people had been touched with revulsion by the genocide of the Final Solution and, no doubt, with guilt because of the historical legacy of injustice to and oppression of African Americans. This sensibility was a foundation upon which the federal government, especially its executive and judicial branches, was willing to speak out and act in behalf of civil rights.

On June 25, 1941, President Franklin D. Roosevelt signed Executive Order No. 8802 establishing the Fair Employment Practices Committee. In 1944 the Supreme Court, in the *Smith* v. *Allwright* decision, struck down the so-called white primary. And in 1946 with the *Morgan* v. *Virginia* decision the Supreme Court voided a statute requiring racial segregation in interstate as well as intrastate commerce. In this same year President Harry S Truman acted to legitimate the role and responsibility of the federal government in safeguarding individual freedoms for all citizens by issuing Executive Order No. 9808 establishing a National Committee on Civil Rights. President Truman's Executive Order No. 9981, on July 26, 1948, ordered the desegregation of the armed services; and later that year the Supreme Court in *Shelly* v. *Kraemer* and *Hurd* v. *Hodge* declared that housing covenants designed to restrict ownership of property or residence according to race could not be legally enforced.[10] These developments combined to provide the African American community with a deepened sense of a common fate, some basis of hope in continued struggle and protest, reinforcement of a group rationale of common aspiration, and a moral claim to redress of grievances.

Groundwork for many of the above changes in the major institutional structures of work, enfranchisement, housing, and other aspects of civil liberties and civil rights had been laid in previous decades by the evolving alliance between the African and Jewish American communities. In spite of these institutional adjustments, the favorable stance toward the civil rights of African Americans by some in national positions of leadership throughout the 1940s, wartime prosperity, and the highly visible social mobility to middle-class affluence and respectability of other ethnic and immigrant groups, the African American community remained substantially unaffected and largely unnoticed in its almost pariah status in American society. And, most remarkably, in spite of continued injustices and inequities — and no substantive change in the relative status of the minority group — there still was little evidence of organized militancy by the African American community during this period.[11] The stage was set, however, for serious organized protest and intense militancy.

STATUS OF THE SPECIAL RELATIONSHIP

The evidence at hand suggests that a definite lull took place in the growth of the alliance between the African and Jewish American communities during the latter part of the 1930s and the early half of the 1940s. It cannot be concluded that a reduction in the strength of the previously established bond between these two minority communities occurred, nor is there any overwhelming reason to conclude that there was any perceptible strengthening of the coalition formation between them as a consequence of this period of temporary inactivity.

However, one conclusive development, important in its implications for coalition formation in succeeding decades, took place in August 1945. This was the formation of a team of lawyers and other specialists from the NAACP, the American Jewish Congress, the American Jewish Committee, and the Anti-Defamation League to pursue to the bitter end the so-called Educational Strategy first succinctly enunciated during the early 1930s.[12] This gambit of the alliance culminated eventually in the historic 1954 *Brown* v. *Board of Education of Topeka* Supreme Court decision on public school desegregation.

Inactivity in the growth of the alliance between the Jewish and African American communities during most of this decade does not seem to be caused by factors or forces imminent in the process of coalition formation. Rather, this apparent lull is best understood as a reasonable by-product of the operations of that massive matrix of external forces peculiar to the times.

These external forces originated in both foreign and domestic sources. They included the national role of the United States as the Arsenal of Democracy and the pursuit of the Four Freedoms — a utopian view of the world which was a central part of the legacy of President Roosevelt. The malevolence of the Holocaust and the turbulent conditions surrounding the creation of the Jewish state of Israel were of signal importance also. The drama of the civil rights struggle as engaged in by both federal and state governments as part of the Fair Deal of President Truman was of immeasurable significance domestically, as was the frenzy engendered by the nation's obsession with Communist subversion and with the appearances of patriotism and loyalty. Furthermore, controversies erupted surrounding the implementation of the Truman Doctrine with its objectives of relief and, then, of rehabilitation of the nations of Europe. There also were disturbing national and international crises emerging out of two encounters with the power of the Soviet Union in which military force was not directly involved — dealing with Russian power through the intermediary of the Chinese civil war and the Korean conflict. All of these domestic and international events made up a substantial part of the contextual reality — that massive matrix of external factors and forces — against which the apparent lull in the alliance process between the African and Jewish American communities during the 1940s must be appreciated.

There is grave risk in interpreting accurately the significance of this dormancy in the process of alliance between the two minority communities during this critical period of war, the dilemmas of peace, and national recovery. It is clear, nevertheless, that the Jewish American community had attained a structural position of social eminence as well as countervailing power in local and national centers of policy determination and decision making. It is equally clear, on the other hand, that the status of the African American community remained largely that of an impotent pariah, a minority group chronically and conspicuously deprived relative to almost all other racial and ethnic communities.

The consciousness of and sensitivity to (certainly for the Jewish American community and, undoubtedly, also for the African American community) the impact of international events upon minority group status in the United States — given the nation's new superpower status — had been immeasurably heightened during the 1940s. The apparent lull, or period of lassitude, in the historical process of alliance between the two minority communities during this period is best understood, therefore, as an adjustment stage that permitted the factoring of international developments into this particular matrix of coalition formation.

By the early 1950s, however, this period of dormancy in the process of coalition formation ended with some of the clearest affirmations ever of public or official recognition of the alliance between the African and Jewish American communities. This formal recognition is to be found in the annual reports between 1953 and 1955 of the National Jewish Community Relations Council (NJCRC) — the coordinating group including all of the Jewish organizations, both national and local, dealing with American domestic affairs.[13]

A path now may be tentatively sketched of the historical process of coalition formation and alliance between the African and Jewish American communities. First, between approximately 1890 and 1919, there was the discovery or exploratory stage. The collective behaviors of the two minority communities during this first stage may be described, generally, as driven by a growing consciousness, or an initial awakening, of a sense of mutual interests and the groping exploration of concerted actions.

The alliance process then evolved, between approximately 1920 and 1939, through a rather clear-cut bonding stage, demonstrating the potential of the two minority communities for coalition-like behavior on a variety of public policy issues. During this second stage of the alliance there emerged, clearly, evidence of a lack of parity in the alliance between the allies or partners. Symptomatic of this disparity and revealing evidence of possible misalliance between the African and Jewish American communities are the experiences encountered in the application of the strategies of being of use and the politics of the arts and, as well, in the shrill allegations and denials of endemic anti-Semitism in the urban sectors of the African American community.

The third stage of the alliance process (between 1940 and 1953) of the African and Jewish American communities involves two distinct phases. First, between approximately 1940 and 1945, there was a phase of quiescence, ideological confusion, and adjustment. Potentially damaging strains and tensions to coalition formation — a legacy of the late 1930s — had surfaced between the two minority communities centering around charges of anti-Semitism in the African American community, the alleged use by the Jewish American community of double standards of group (ethical, moral, and racial) judgments to give meaning to the reality of events of the time, and increasing intergroup competition throughout local and national settings for hierarchical position and autonomy in joint activities.

The second phase of this third stage of alliance, from about 1946 to 1953, is best described as a rapprochement period culminating with formal, public recognition of the coalition between the African and

Jewish American communities. This official recognition and resumption of concerted action by the coalition or alliance is interpreted as a prelude essential for the mobilization of both minority communities for the coordinated militancy demanded by the looming civil rights movement.

NOTES

1. Johnson, *History of the Jews,* pp. 460–61. An excellent description of the dynamics of this transformation is provided by Arthur Hertzberg, *The Jews in America: Four Centuries of an Uneasy Encounter — A History* (New York: Simon and Schuster, 1989), especially Chapter 16, "FDR: The Benevolent King of the Jews."

2. Feuerlicht, *Fates of the Jews,* pp. 139–41. See Chapter V for a description of modern Zionism. Also, Robert G. Weisbord, *African Zion: The Attempt to Establish A Jewish Colony in the East African Protectorate, 1903–1905* (Philadelphia: The Jewish Publication Society of America, 1968); Weisbord and Stein, *Bittersweet Encounter.* The definitive historical analysis of the Zionist movement, in my opinion, is to be found in Johnson, *History of the Jews,* especially pp. 375–421. For a succinct description of the beginnings, the creation, and the Jewish American response to Zionism see Hertzberg, *Jews in America,* pp. 84, 165.

3. Berson, *Negroes and the Jews,* p. 108.

4. Ibid., p. 108. The ideological disarray of the Jewish American community at this time is described in some detail too by Feuerlicht, *Fates of the Jews,* pp. 132–39.

5. See Feuerlicht, *Fates of the Jews,* pp. 132–33. There are any number of reputable accounts and in-depth analyses of the Jewish genocide in Europe. Especially helpful to me have been Lucy Davidowicz, "The Holocaust Was Unique in Intent, Scope, and Effect," in *The Center Magazine* XIV:4 (July/August 1981): 46–64; Raul Hilberg, *The Destruction of the European Jews* (Chicago: Quadrangle Books, 1961); and Johnson, *History of the Jews,* Part Six, pp. 423–517.

6. Questions such as how Israel was established, what existed in Palestine before its establishment, what justified its establishment, and what forces brought it about are beyond the scope of this book. For an examination of these questions about Israel as the state of the Jewish people see Johnson, *History of the Jews,* Part Seven, pp. 519–83; and Johnson, *History of the Modern World,* Chapter 14, especially pp. 480–87. For an incisive analysis from what may be called a Middle East or Arab perspective see Edward W. Said, "An Ideology of Difference," in *Writing and Difference,* ed. Henry Louis Gates, Jr. (Chicago: University of Chicago Press, 1986), pp. 38–58.

7. The dynamics of this process of brokerage is described in some detail by Feuerlicht, *Fates of the Jews,* pp. 139–50.

8. Cabell Phillips, *The 1940s* (New York: Macmillan Publishing Co., 1975), p. 68.

9. A fairly detailed account of the dynamics of this attempt by the United States and British governments, media, and armed services to reduce the African American serviceman in World War II especially (but also in World War I) to chronic subservience, dehumanization, and degradation is to be found in Graham Smith, *When Jim Crow Met John Bull: Black American Soldiers in World War II Britain* (New York: St. Martin's Press, 1987).

10. Gustavus Myers, *History of Bigotry in the United States* (New York: Capricorn Books, 1960), pp. 441–42. See also Phillips, *The 1940s,* pp. 345–54.

11. For example, in 1951 an incident took place in Cicero, a suburb of Chicago, Illinois, that attracted national and international attention. A young African American professional family moved into largely working-class, all-European American Cicero. Antiracial feelings exploded, and the National Guard had to be mobilized to restore order. See Myers, *History of Bigotry,* pp. 446–47.

12. Berson, *Negroes and the Jews,* pp. 96–97; and Kaufman, *Broken Alliance,* p. 91.

13. Hertzberg, *Jews in America,* pp. 334–37.

5

Schooling and Civil Rights: 1954–1965

The Supreme Court decision of *Brown* v. *Board of Education,* 347 U.S. 483, handed down in 1954, overturned the pernicious separate-but-equal doctrine of the 1896 *Plessy* v. *Ferguson* decision. This landmark decision was a part of the tenor of major legal changes, especially since World War II, that increasingly reinforced the legitimacy of the hopes and aspirations of the African American community. Instrumentally, this decision (and the implementing decree of 1955) — which mandated a shift in the public system of American schooling from a traditional mode of racial segregation (especially in the South) to one of racial desegregation — focused extraordinary attention throughout the world upon the problem of race in American society and, though devastatingly shocking to some with its implementation phrase of "with deliberate speed," portended the necessity for urgent social change.

Such major legal decisions were necessary but not sufficient to remedy conclusively and immediately those problematic outcomes of over 300 years of exploitation, oppression, and indignity endured uniquely in the United States by those of African descent. There is to be found little evidence that does not at least suggest that officially sanctioned racial segregation and discrimination resulted — individually and collectively — in dehumanization and malevolent injury to all involved in such a social arrangement. Thus, it is not overreaching to state that by the mid-1950s the ultimate end of law — that is, justice (and here I include the reversal of discrimination, redress, and restitution) — had become the collective obsession of the African American community.

This passion was not merely legitimization of the principle of the sanctity of the rule of law for, most importantly, this apparent obsession of the African American community seemed to be increasingly acceptable to the European American majority. By the mid-1950s — a decade that has been described as a time of self-indulgence and prosperity

— almost imperceptibly, substantial changes seem to have taken place in the national culture that would have significant implications both for the structure of political, economic, and social opportunities for the African American community and for the alliance between the African and Jewish American communities.

Exercising, rather than influencing, national leadership had become the predominant mission of the Jewish American community by the time of the *Brown* decisions. The Jewish American community had become, in effect, a minority group that had "arrived" because it had become consolidated in that central core of power in America that was responsible for dispensing or rectifying deliberate, official actions of historic racial injustice.[1]

Thus, the *Brown* desegregation decision contributed immensely to the triggering of what can be called the "nationalization of civil liberties and civil rights" between 1954 and 1965. The institutional and spatial terms of the civil rights movement, in other words, were to be no longer localized largely by place in the deep and upper southern states; the entire nation — the North, the Midwest, and the West — and most of the institutionalized aspects of American society now were to become stages of conflict. And, as will be developed later, this linking of change in the legal framework sanctifying the functioning of the racially segregated public schooling system with the advent of militant mass movements of protest was not fortuitous.

The foreign and domestic contexts between 1954 and 1965, within which the African and Jewish American alliance had to revitalize the struggle for civil rights, were replete with complexity and perplexity. First, in the international context, the birth of the so-called Third World was heralded by the African-Asian Conference at Bandung, Indonesia, in April 1955. This development was a part of the exit of a coterie of European nations from an antiquated form of colonial imperialism and the transfer from colonial rule to nominal independence of formerly exploited and oppressed African, Asian, and Middle Eastern peoples. Second, cold war problems developed concerning the management of the consequences of the partition of the Indian subcontinent into the Islamic nation of Pakistan and the essentially Hindu nation of India. Third, problems were created by the 1956–1957 invasion of Egypt by the combined British, French, and Israeli forces and the emergence of the Palestine Liberation Organization (PLO) out of the immediate issues of Middle East boundaries and refugees. Finally, the world-threatening issue of the control of atomic power emerged with its attendant ideological and military problems.[2]

Domestically, the nation was embroiled in a struggle for power between the left and right wings of national political factions involving accusations of treason, as embodied in that movement labeled McCarthyism. The nation also experienced tensions between local and national power and authority — reflected in the Little Rock, Arkansas, school desegregation crisis — that were so salient during the Eisenhower presidency.[3] The Montgomery Bus Boycott in December 1955 signaled the onset of insurgency from the African American community. The election and subsequent assassination of John F. Kennedy, the first U.S. president of the Roman Catholic faith, may be identified as the beginning of a period of violence the variety of which had hardly been witnessed before in the nation. The so-called War on Poverty, conceived under the administration of President Kennedy but conducted largely under the leadership of President Lyndon B. Johnson, was an integral part of the process of nationalization of civil liberties and civil rights occurring during the latter half of the 1950s and continuing into the exuberance and turbulence that marked the nation during most of the 1960s. Finally, according to Feuerlicht,[4] the nation experienced the death of the "Old Left" and the birth of the "New Left," the latter a mass movement comprising essentially European American, middle-class college students (or young people of college age) but including a conspicuous number of Jewish Americans.

Out of the above situational context erupted the thrust of what came to be called the civil rights movement that was to alter the fundamental identity of both the African American community and that of American society. From this thrust emerged that which earlier I called the nationalization of civil liberties and civil rights.

In examining aspects of this massive process of social change in the remainder of this chapter, at least three facts must be kept in mind. First, the litigative advocacy strategy — first hit upon during the second decade of the century during the exploratory and formative stages of the alliance between the African and Jewish American communities — was to be continued. Second, there was apparent agreement within the African and Jewish American alliance for continuity of the so-called educational strategy first succinctly formulated during the 1930s in its bonding stage.[5] Inducing change in the racial character of the public schooling system was to be a primary goal of the alliance.

Finally, there was continuity also in the lack of status parity between those represented in the alliance — the African and Jewish American communities. On the one hand the status of the Jewish American community in the nation at this time, by and large, was nonproblematic or at least was characterized by what may be called benign acceptance. Stated differently, while that certain unique nervousness or form of American ambivalence toward Jews held by most other American citizens remained, it had begun very early in the history of the nation,[6] and its intensity at this particular point in time seemed to have lessened considerably. On the other hand, the status of the African American community in the nation remained, largely, that of malignant stigmatization. The continuity of this lack of status parity between the two minority communities — and between their representatives who made up a formal coalition of unequal partners — will be seen to play a significant role in the looming struggle for prevailing control of the alliance.

THE POLITICS OF SCHOOLING AND RACISM

The schooling system is the most powerful instrument a society possesses for fashioning its members in its own image.[7] Recognition of this potential for social power and social control may account for much of the conflict observed historically (or in the analytic examination of the origin, evolution, and function of America's public schooling system) in and about the preschool, elementary, secondary, and higher education levels of the nation's educational institutions.[8] The nonpublic (parochial, private or elite, independent, or so-called nongovernment schooling arrangements) schooling systems are another matter. However, the apparent effects of these alternative schooling systems were to merely enhance the fundamental societal consequences of the nation's public schooling system, that is, the perpetuation through a medley of group competition and conflict, strains, and tensions of a societal structure of privilege, inequality, and domination.

For the purpose at hand, then, emphasis is placed upon the basic function of the public educational institution, or the schooling system, to reproduce and legitimate social inequality; to resist change, to remain essentially stable, or to maintain an existing societal arrangement of privilege and domination. In other words, the importance of the proposition cannot be overstated that the public schooling system of America is best viewed, when looking at the interrelations of a particular set of minority communities existing under the hegemony of a superordinate group, as a mechanism of social control operating to maintain and perpetuate the existing racial and social class structure of hierarchy and inequality.[9]

Ultimately, therefore, the total system of schooling in the United States, in terms of understanding the evolution of the African and Jewish

American coalition, is best treated as a political process. That is, one of the American schooling system's most prominent features — throughout its metamorphoses from the common school paradigm of the colonial period to the mass, public, compulsory, bureaucratic paradigm of today — is its potential for becoming an object of conflict for societal groupings (religious, class, language, racial, and cultural) struggling to obtain, and to maintain, social power and social control.

There is hardly any controversy in U.S. history that takes temporal precedence over that about the type and amount of schooling for those of African descent in America. This controversy continues to this day. Read closely the historical record shows that schooling controversies involving the fates of African Americans tended almost always to be resolved through myriad subterfuges so as to relegate their rights, privileges, and welfare to subordination to and difference from those of European Americans. Bullock concludes, for instance, that "By the close of the nineteenth century, Northern educators had made a crucial decision. They had decided to sell the idea of Negro education to white Southerners by sacrificing the principle of racial equality."[10] This decision, no doubt, contributed largely to the legitimation of the industrial educational philosophy of Booker T. Washington.

The evidence is overwhelming that untold costs, monetary and nonmonetary, to all citizens of the nation have been and continue to be paid as a direct consequence of this institutional racism buried in what is, essentially, our national educational policy. Furthermore, the past and present vulnerability of the African American community in its quest for equality and justice reasonably may be said to be caused in large part by the cumulated effect of the use of this educational policy. There is little hyperbole in stating that in the implementation of this essentially national educational policy access to schooling for African Americans was used as a pawn. It became a negotiable power of exchange or commodity for bargaining between competing European American elites to insure the maintenance of structures of racial inequality while insuring the denial of humanity to, as well as violating the civil liberties and rights of, the African American minority group.

It must be noted here that this peculiar nexus of the African American community with the schooling system did not burden the Jewish American community. For it, unlike the Roman Catholics of America, early decided not to develop a parallel nonpublic system of schooling. Rather, the Jewish American community, in large part, deliberately decided to avoid the creation of a separate schooling system, electing rather to concentrate upon using the relative openness of the public educational institution as a vehicle of Americanization, assimilation, and social mobility. Thus, the two minority communities from the reality of historical experiences had to attach critically different meanings to the politics of schooling in America.

It follows, therefore, that early in the formation of the coalition between the African and Jewish American communities the blatant racial inequality inherent in the American schooling system, especially as practiced in the South, was selected as a prime target for concerted action. The litigative advocacy strategy was combined with the educational strategy for the purpose of obtaining two tactical objectives: to demonstrate, first, the virtual impossibility of implementation of the doctrine of equal but separate schooling and, second, to then decisively destroy the legality of racial segregation as schooling policy.

Note should be made here of the fact that prior to the crystallization of the educational strategy in the 1930s by the African and Jewish American alliance, securing relief from the injustices of the schooling system had been an important objective of the African American community. Beginning in 1885 it brought legal actions throughout the nation, but largely in the South, to secure relief from educational constraint and inequity imposed by the *Civil Rights Cases of 1883*. A record of this is provided by Bullock.[11]

However, the critical legal attacks essential for the first prong of the educational strategy — to demonstrate the fatal defect of the separate but equal doctrine — began earnestly in 1935 and substantially were effected during the latter half of the 1940s.[12] Now was the time, between approximately 1946 and 1951, to turn to the issue of the legitimation of racial desegregation in schooling as calculatedly designed in the second prong of the educational strategy. The 1954 Supreme Court decision of *Brown* v. *Board of Education* marked the end of this phase of the educational strategy with its symbolic meaning of destroying the policy of racial segregation in schooling.[13] It marked, as well, a concrete victory for the power of coalition building, the result of an alliance in the politics of power largely between two minority groups — the African and Jewish American communities.

One of the apexes of solidarity (the other apex occurred during the 1920s) between the African and Jewish American communities occurred during that period between the end of World War II and the handing down in 1954 of the *Brown* decision.[14] In other words, the transactions and interchanges between these two minority communities, involving processes of bargaining, negotiating, cooperating and even conflicting, were most evident and at heightened intensity during this time. There can be no reasonable denial of the concerted actions — the strategic and tactical conduct — of the African and Jewish American alliance. What is now established conclusively is the particularity of that interactive behavior in the coalition-formation process between these two minority groups: the existence of specific goals, conditions, and reasons for the coalition; the undeniable presence of understandings and mutually agreed upon policy; and the concrete result of their concerted actions. With the *Brown* decision, the African and Jewish American alliance demonstrated the efficacy of the power of politics in the politics of race.

Victories are deceptive always. Securing a favorable outcome in the *Brown* decision brought with it, also, at least two unintended consequences for the African and Jewish American alliance. First, as a result of failure in the complicated attempts to implement the *Brown* decision between 1954 and approximately 1965, clear indications emerged within the African American community of increased disenchantment, even a disturbing level of collective cynicism, with the way things were in the United States. It had become conspicuously clear — at least to the African American community — that school desegregation was meeting inexplicable difficulties in achievement. Moreover, if by some miracle racial desegregation was achieved in the nation's schooling system, few reassurances were seen that it would contribute conclusively and immediately to the attainment of the ultimate goals of equality and justice for the African American community. The doubts circulating almost constantly within the myriad circles and levels of an oppressed, degraded, and exploited minority community — about those myths in American culture that portrayed the schooling system as a ladder of mobility for the individual and the group and about the alleged efficacy of legal action to achieve justice and equality — came, in an existential sense, to be confirmed by the reality of their perceived situation.

The second unintended consequence of the *Brown* decision had to do with planting the seed of disillusionment with, or presaging a serious rupture of, what appeared to be the successfully evolved alliance between the African and Jewish American communities. At issue was simply the fact that the legal authority for an injurious public policy had been undermined or destroyed, but the historically grounded consequences of that policy — the racist structures and processes of degradation, inequality, and injustice — continued to give insult and injury.

The African American community, after at least 30 years of sustained court litigation and after the complete acceptance since the end of the institution of slavery of the national ideology of education as a means of succor for massive individual and collective damage, had secured no reasonable relief. The stage was set, therefore, for turning to alternative, and even noninstitutional, ways of securing the ultimate goals of racial equality and justice in America.

Serious disaffection developed about those fundamental understandings underlying the apparent consensus held by the African and Jewish American alliance. Of these flawed understandings two were of primary importance for the continued unity of the coalition. First, serious doubts were raised about the tactical efficiency of the strategy of legal advocacy and persuasion over that of the possible use of direct, confrontational actions. Second, the proposition or understanding that gave priority to the public schooling system rather than the political and economic systems as the proper target within the national arena of public interest for changing the structures of injustice and inequality was challenged severely.

Thus, from these ideological seams of skepticism within the African and Jewish American alliance — as well as from intracommunal tensions resulting from class, regional, and international developments impinging in quite different ways upon both minority communities — the stage was set also for a new element in the diversity and discontinuity, richness and fragmentation, fecundity and fluidity of the character of the civil rights struggle.

THE POLITICS OF PROTEST:
THE CIVIL RIGHTS MOVEMENT

Of equal importance to the politics of schooling and racism for the nationalization of civil liberties and civil rights was the dynamics of the politics of protest, that collective behavior manifested in social movement form, between approximately 1954 and 1965, commonly labeled the civil rights movement.[15] The error must not be made here of merely equating the so-called civil rights struggle with those activities of protest usually described as occurring during the latter half of the 1950s and the first half of the 1960s. There would be little overreaching, in truth, if the entire history of those of African descent in the United States is called a civil rights movement. Our chief concern in this chapter, however, is with only that phase of the general historical process commonly called the civil rights movement, which is bounded, approximately, by the years 1954 and 1965.

In addition, the civil rights movement, in both its general historical sense or its particular sense of concern as in this chapter, is not held to be synonymous with civil rights organizations. Clark observes, for instance,

That the civil rights movement had its own historic and impersonal momentum, responsive to deep and powerful economic and international events and political and ideological forces beyond the control of individuals, agencies, or perhaps even individual governments. In fact, the uncontrollable power and momentum of the civil rights movement impelled it to create the necessary machinery, organizations, and leaders.[16]

Identification of those voluntary associations seriously committed to the struggle for civil liberties and civil rights is essential, nevertheless, for understanding the civil rights movement in either its historical or particular senses. A listing of selected organizations, from both the African and Jewish American communities that were prominently involved at some time between 1775 and 1967 in the struggle for human rights, that is, civil liberties and civil rights, is found in the Appendix.

The collective disaffection and disenchantment with the pragmatic consequences of the *Brown* decision for schooling desegregation has been described above in the section on the politics of schooling and racism. As a consequence of such endemic disaffection, that essential consensus about ends and means — which had been so diligently cultivated by the leadership elites and prominent civil rights organizations of the African American community since at least the 1920s, and by the alliance — was made perilous. In fact, the dissolution of this consensus proceeded rapidly.

The profound resentment and discontent permeating the masses of the African American community manifested themselves in at least two important responses. And, as is shown later, these developments of response to collective discontent and resentment will prove to be of profound significance for the alliance of the Jewish and African American communities, for neither response was apparently consonant precisely with any corresponding development in the Jewish American community.

First, emerging from the masses of the African American community was a serious challenge to the legitimacy of the leadership of those organizations (the NAACP and the National Urban League) traditionally in the vanguard of the civil rights struggle. This challenge was reminiscent of the earlier challenge made during the 1920s by the Garvey movement to the leadership of the NAACP, the National Urban League, and the artistic and intellectual elites of the Harlem Renaissance. At issue in both instances were different immediate goals, tactical weapons, sources of leadership, and organizational resources. And, while both challenges were responses to a massive contagion of discontent, they attacked not only the entrenched interests of the European American majority but, as well, the self-serving interests of the African American middle class and the Jewish American community in the civil rights struggle.

African American ministers traditionally were not highly visible in the leadership cadres of the major civil rights organizations, yet they had been held to be targets of suspicion by the dominant European American majority since the revolts of 1821 and 1831 led by Denmark Vesey and Nat Turner.[17] Now, with the emergence from the depths of the African American community of mass resistance and organized sustained protest between 1954 and 1965, a rich and creative source of leadership talent was uncovered from among the ministers and the cohorts of college students within the African American community. This was a most disturbing, and even shocking, discovery for the Jewish and African American alliance.

Unable to effect significant reform of the traditional civil rights organizations, this new leadership cadre — composed largely of ministers, college students, and disgruntled and idealistic elements of the middle classes — created organizations such as the Congress of Racial Equality (CORE), the Southern Christian Leadership Conference (SCLC), and the Student Nonviolent Coordinating Committee (SNCC) and, as well, developed new tactics, for example, passive or nonviolent resistance, "jail, no bail," and the use of music to ensure participatory unity,[18] to respond to the swelling resentment surfacing out of the African American community.

With this literal shunting aside of the traditional civil rights organizations and their leadership elites came a crisis of identity and meaning for the African and Jewish American alliance. A substantial change had occurred in the character of participation by the masses and the idealistic and disgruntled middle-class members of the African American community, somewhat bolstered apparently by favorable nationwide sentiment, in the civil rights struggle, and neither ally in the alliance was comfortable with this development. Before this time, the control of the civil rights struggle and its organizational agencies had been monopolized largely by the intellectual and artistic elites of the African American community, and especially as embodied eventually in the African and Jewish American alliance. The African American masses had played primarily a supportive and, perhaps, even a largely resigned participatory role in the litigative and educational strategies of earlier decades or in previous phases of the evolving alliance between the Jewish and African American communities.

Now, out of the deep well of massive collective discontent and alienation, aggressive initiative was being uncovered out of that large stratum of working class, religiously oriented, family oriented majority of the African American community, the stratum of the so-called urban underclass, and the stratum of youth involved in schooling and the institutions of higher education bolstered, almost always, by disillusioned elements of the middle class. These strata, heretofore underutilized, provided the new cadre of leadership with the opportunity for a systematic mass campaign of organized protest.[19] In brief, it would seem that the African American community had acquired at this time, and to some extent largely independent of the African and Jewish American alliance, a mechanism of protest with its own leadership sensitive to particularistic needs, a sense of common fate, a basis for hope, common aspirations, and, above all, a moral claim to redress of grievances.

The groundswell of discontent and alienation emerging from the masses, and other elements of the heretofore accommodating spaces, of the African American community contributed fundamentally to the emergence of the politics of protest. Nontraditional voluntary associations such as SCLC, SNCC, CORE, and the Nation of Islam were at hand to drive this groundswell with or without the cooperation of traditional organizations such as the NAACP and the National Urban League or the traditional leadership cadres and, to some extent, regardless of the African and Jewish American alliance. In a sense, this minority community had turned inward, demonstrating a predisposition to placing primary reliance upon its own resources to carry out its struggle for equality and justice. This was a portentous message sent to the African and Jewish American alliance.

The second response to the massive collective discontent and alienation swelling out of the African American community was a profound change in the quality of the struggle for civil rights. Without rejecting entirely customary and institutionalized modes of seeking redress — such as litigation, electoral politics, legislative changes, educational attainment, and persuasion — reliance, most innovatively, began to be placed upon noninstitutional modes of action. Civil disobedience, noncompliance, agitation, noncooperation, and even subversion began to become favored weapons of the politics of protest. Examples of these nontraditional actions include, for instance, the Montgomery Bus Boycott, the sit-ins at public facilities, freedom rides, the drives for voting registration throughout the South, demonstrations about housing and work largely in metropolitan areas, and the March on Washington.

A striking feature of these tactical actions was the undercurrent of rancor, hostility, and belligerence associated with them. This new quality of the civil rights struggle was of grave concern both to the African and

Jewish American alliance and, because of their pervasive coverage by the medium of television, the U.S. government. Before this time in the history of those of African descent in the United States the option of violence, revolt, insurrection, and revolution had never been considered a realistic means of changing the social order, largely, no doubt, because of their being a numerical and highly visible minority group. Yet, paradoxically, both the institutional and noninstitutional modes of protest seemed to have significant impact upon the civil rights policies of the presidential administrations of John F. Kennedy and Lyndon B. Johnson and, as well, upon the dynamics of the major political parties. Such responses to the evolving militancy of the civil rights struggle contributed significantly to the nationalization of the struggle for civil rights between 1954 and 1965.[20]

Thus, out of the mass discontent of the African American community with the unfulfilled promises and expectations of the *Brown* decision, and the politics of schooling that emerged from it, the civil rights movement was catapulted into national prominence. As noted, this process of nationalization of the civil rights and civil liberties movement between approximately 1954 and 1965 had grave implications for the continuing cohesion of the African and Jewish American alliance. Several factors combined to plant seeds of discord within the alliance: the turning inward of the African American community for new sources of leadership and its adoption of nontraditional modes of conducting the civil rights struggle; changing perceptions of individual and group identities within the African American community; the lingering legacies within the African and Jewish American coalition of latent problems of dissidence; and the increased preoccupation of the Jewish American community with the crises of the nation of Israel.

The intrinsic character of the alliance between these two minority communities was altered by the difficult decisions made over several decades by the Jewish American community to that troublesome issue of the relation between the Jewish Diaspora and the state of Israel. As commonly understood, the resolution of this issue committed the Jewish American community to the provision of financial and political support (that is, essentially with the federal government) to the state of Israel but conceded, reluctantly, any determinative influence on the use to which such support should be put.[21] This meant, in effect, that the primary goal orientation of the Jewish American community had shifted from a now unnecessary concern with collective survival and adjustment in the United States (and thereby reasonably including its strategic partnership with the African American community in the civil rights struggle) to the mission of guaranteeing the security and survival of the state of Israel.

In fulfilling this entente the Jewish American community emerged as a most potent supporter of that special relationship evolved — especially in the area of foreign policy — between the United States and Israel. The precise nature of this special relationship is unclear, but it is usually explained officially as serving the vital interests of the United States — especially in the Middle East — resulting in the close strategic and political ties of the two nations. One dimension of this particular aspect of the vital interest is the United States' "longstanding commitment to maintain Israel's military superiority in the Middle East."[22] As an ally Israel consistently arranges, largely through the influence of the Jewish American community, to receive preferential treatment or special favors (for example, outright grants rather than loans as is the case of other allies) in the areas of economic and military aid and assistance.[23] Thus, this growing preoccupation of the Jewish American community with the welfare of the state of Israel, and the correlative relations of Israel with some of the developing African and Arab nation states, became one of the concerns that severely strained the solidarity of the African and Jewish American alliance.

A harsh rupture between the major parties in the coalition seemed inevitable. In the evolutionary process of the civil rights movement — with the subsequent emergence of the ideologies of separatism and "Black Power"; with the transition of legitimacy from the doctrine of passive or nonviolent resistance to that sanctioning of the use of the weapons of violence; with the development (especially through the diligence of the Jewish American community) of a special relationship between the state of Israel and the United States in the foreign policy area — rupture of the alliance of the African and Jewish American communities became a certainty.

NOTES

1. Johnson, *History of the Jews*, p. 567.
2. Johnson, *History of the Modern World*, Chapter 10; and Hans J. Morgenthau, *Purpose of American Politics* (New York: Knopf, 1960), especially Part III.
3. Morgenthau, *Purpose of American Politics*, pp. 143–57.
4. Feuerlicht, *Fates of the Jews*, p. 147.
5. The educational strategy, first succinctly formulated early in the 1930s, was designed to test the strength of the "separate but equal" doctrine enunciated in the *Plessy* v. *Ferguson* decision of 1896. It called for the legal attack of racial segregation

in the schooling system at its point of greatest vulnerability — the point where no claim of "separate but equal" could be reasonably made and where no promise of equalization could be realistically given. See Bullock, *History of Negro Education*, p. 226.

6. Arthur Hertzberg, *The Jews in America* (New York: Simon and Schuster, 1989), pp. 88–89.

7. This insight is developed most completely by Durkheim. See Emile Durkheim, *The Evolution of Educational Thought*, trans. Peter Collins (London: Routledge & Kegan Paul, 1977). Schooling is considered to be the "deliberate, systematic, and sustained effort to transmit, evoke, or acquire knowledge, values, attitudes, skills, and sensibilities (and the results of that effort)," Lawrence A. Cremin, "The Family as Educator: Some Comments on the Recent Historiography," in Hope Jensen Leichter, ed., *The Family as Educator* (New York: Columbia University Press, 1974), p. 86.

8. A vast literature explores this topic of conflict over the control of the schooling system. But, see Laurence A. Cremin, *The Transformation of the Schools* (New York: Knopf, 1961).

9. This perspective follows largely the approaches of Pierre Bourdieu and Jean-Claude Passeron, *Reproduction: In Education, Society and Culture* (London: Sage Publications, 1977); and Samuel Bowles and Herbert Gintis, *Schooling in Capitalist America* (New York: Basic Books, Inc., 1976). For a development of the notion of domination see Trent Schroyer, *The Critique of Domination* (Boston: Beacon Press, 1973).

10. Bullock, *History of Negro Education*, p. 93.

11. Ibid., pp. 214–21.

12. The legal actions included in this phase of the educational strategy are described by Bullock, *History of Negro Education*, pp. 26–231. For the pivotal role of the Jewish American community, and especially that of the Commission of Law and Social Action deliberately created for this purpose by the American Jewish Congress, see Berson, *Negroes and the Jews*, pp. 110–11.

13. A legal and social science background for this second prong of the educational strategy of the African and Jewish American alliance and some analysis of its consequences up to the middle of the 1960s is provided by Bullock, *History of Negro Education*, pp. 231–65.

14. Berson, *Negroes and the Jews*, pp. 96–111. Concerted actions of the alliance, including the cooperative publication of annual reports and the continuous monitoring and investigations of activities considered germane to civil rights, are noted not only in instances involving the schooling system but in almost all other areas of the public interest.

15. By social movement is meant "that type of behavior in which a large number of participants consciously attempt to change existing institutions and establish a new order of life." This definition, as well as its theoretic foundations, is provided in Rhoda Lois Blumberg, *Civil Rights: The 1960s Freedom Struggle* (Boston: G. K. Hall & Co., 1984), pp. 167, 168–77. However, according to Williams, *Mutual Accommodation*, p. 218,

> Social movements of dissent and reform may accept most of the values and norms of the larger society in which they rise and confine their activities to

those modes of opposition and advocacy that are institutionalized, e.g., electoral politics, legislative change, judicial proceedings. Often, however, a movement for social change does not initially have acceptance as a legitimate claimant within the established political arena. It then may both advocate and act in terms of alternative or new standards and modes of behavior — civil disobedience, noncompliance, mass agitation, noncooperation, violent opposition, subversion, revolution.

Thus, in accordance with the elaboration by Williams, the civil rights movement as perceived in this work will include both institutionalized as well as noninstitutionalized modes of behavior. For additional specifications of the constructs of social movement, mass movements, and collective behavior see Geschwender, *The Black Revolt,* pp. 2–17; and Ralph H. Turner and Lewis M. Killian, *Collective Behavior* (Englewood Cliffs, NJ: Prentice-Hall, Inc., 1957), Parts Four and Five.

16. Kenneth B. Clark, "The Civil Rights Movement: Momentum and Organization," in Geschwender, ed., *The Black Revolt,* p. 47.

17. Eileen Southern, *The Music of Black Americans: A History* (New York: W. W. Norton & Co., 1983), p. 72.

18. Nonviolent resistance is perceived as types of constraint actions designed to develop countervailing power against the exercise of arbitrary power. For a treatment of such strategy and tactics in collective action such as the civil rights movement see Williams, *Mutual Accommodations,* pp. 215–37. The pioneer in the use of the philosophy of interracial nonviolent direct action among civil rights movement organizations was CORE. See especially Part I of August Meier and Elliot Rudwick, *CORE: A Study In the Civil Rights Movement 1942–1968* (Urbana: University of Illinois Press, 1975); and Paula Giddings, *When and Where I Enter: The Impact of Black Women on Race and Sex in America* (New York: William Morrow, 1984), pp. 279, 283.

19. For a trenchant description of the underrecognized roles of African American women in the civil rights movement see Giddings, *When and Where I Enter.*

20. The role of the federal government in the civil rights movement during the 1950s and 1960s is described in considerable detail in the following works: David J. Garrow, *Bearing the Cross: Martin Luther King, Jr. and the Southern Christian Leadership Conference* (New York: William Morrow, 1986); and Clayborne Carson, *In Struggle: SNCC and the Black Awakening of the 1960s* (Cambridge, MA: Harvard University Press, 1981).

21. Hertzberg, *Jews in America,* pp. 342–43.

22. Eric Schmitt, "$13 Billion Weapons Sale to Saudis Will be Delayed," *The New York Times,* January 5, 1991, Sec. L, p. 5.

23. Treatment of some examples of the special favors accorded the state of Israel by the U.S. government is found in Bernard Gwertzman, "Foreign Aid is Now an Even Tougher Sell," *The New York Times,* March 18, 1986, Sec. 4, p. 1; Clyde H. Farnsworth, "Israel Has A Unique Deal for U.S. Aid," *The New York Times,* September 23, 1990, International Section, p. 18; David K. Shipler, "For Israel and U.S., A Growing Military Partnership," *The New York Times,* March 15, 1987, Sec. E, p. 1; and Elaine Sciolino, "Religious Schools Get U.S. Aid Abroad," *The New York Times,* January 24, 1988, p. 6.

6

The Black Power
Movement: 1966–1979

The African and Jewish American alliance properly celebrated its achievements of significant civil rights reform during the decades of the 1950s and 1960s. These reform results were, in a sense, impressive, and they demonstrated the efficacy of coalition politics for minority groups at the national level. Moreover, they epitomized the ideals of cooperation and concerted action between minority communities within the pervasive racist organization of American society. While reaching these achievements, however, it became clear that at least one of the objectives of the coalition — obtaining equality, justice, and, perhaps, even redress for the historical victimization of the African American minority — had not been reached (certainly from the perspective of a significant part of that complex, diverse mosiac making up the African American community).

It must be understood, nevertheless, that over the past two decades, or since the end of World War II, the African and Jewish American alliance had been the major catalyst, largely through use of the legal system, for a massive racial desegregation process in the military or armed services, amateur and professional athletics or sports, entertainment, and schooling.[1] With such profound change, however, those ultimate goals of equality, justice, and redress for the African American minority continued to be perceived as elusive; and endemic discontent seemed not only to persist but to increase over the continued negative identity or stigmatized image, the inferior relative status, and the marginal dependency of the African American community in American society. Progress had been made toward equality and justice for the minority group, but, as has been seen, significant elements of the African American community perceived it to be still suffering, and unreasonably so, under the undeniable and unique burden of the culturally transmitted or inherited legacy of past neglect and degradation, calculated restrictions, lack of opportunity, and willful exploitation. Apparently it was believed that "progress" was no excuse, at this time, for continued denial of full constitutional and human rights.

Nevertheless, while achieving some progress toward racial equality and justice by the African and Jewish American alliance, it became clear to close observers that a shifting of collective goals and purposes of the two minority communities had taken place as a part of the coalitional process itself. This transformation of the elemental understandings and expectations, the essential rationale, for the alliance threatened its effectiveness, if not its continuity. Contradictions that may have always existed between the disparate as well as mutual interests of the African and Jewish American communities, and which had tended heretofore always to be muted, now became problematic. Achieving victory or some measure of success had exposed or ignited, unintentionally perhaps, forces potentially destructive of the very alliance itself.

Change in goals and means and the rearrangement of priorities guiding policy and action are an inevitable part of the process of a liberating movement such as the civil rights struggle. Such change may be determined both by forces imminent in the process of liberation itself and, at the same time, by situational or contextual forces essentially external to the liberation process. Regardless of source, our concern with this period between 1965 and 1979 is not primarily with isolating the causative determinants of such changes in goals, policies, and priorities but, rather, in identifying accurately those changes perceived or sensed by the major parties in the African and Jewish American alliance.

Thus, the major contour of the external, situational context of the period between approximately 1965 and 1979 within which the liberation process took place must not be ignored. Internationally, the nation pursued its policy of detente[2] as a part of the so-called Cold War, and it was involved in war in Vietnam. The decolonization of so-called Third World nations continued, involving heightening ethnic, racial, and national consciousness throughout the world. There was almost always turmoil in the Middle East, with the state of Israel in constant crisis, thereby accelerating its movement toward favored nation status with, and its dependency upon, the United States. This Middle East turmoil involved, also, the increased international influence, mainly through manipulations involving the oil crises, of Arab nations as well as increased tensions over the issues of refugees and boundaries between the state of Israel and the Palestine Liberation Organization (PLO). In the Far East, there came the recognition by the United States of the People's Republic of China and the looming emergence of Japan as a superpower. Domestically, the so-called War on Poverty was initiated, to be followed by the programs of The Great Society and the scandals of Watergate. The stage was set for the emergence of a serious ideology of difference between the allies comprising the African and Jewish American alliance.

UNCERTAIN AND SHIFTING PRIORITIES

The historic special relationship between the African and Jewish American minority communities was grounded, ultimately, in their objectively similar situations in the United States. The root problem for both minority communities, during the last decade of the nineteenth century but especially during the first two decades of the twentieth century, was that of collective identity in an essentially WASP society. They were perceived generally by the majority of American society to be either distinguishable nonassimilable or nonassimilating minority groups. So the African and Jewish American communities tended to define themselves as threatened or to perceive themselves to be at peril in the nation. They needed each other.

By 1965, however, the objective character of the societal situations of the two minority communities had been radically modified. Most remarkably, the Jewish American community had become almost totally absorbed or assimilated into American society while yet retaining its own distinctive Jewish consciousness. They had "arrived" at the center of American life.[3]

With this transformation of their societal situation came, reasonably, some impetus for redefining the original bases of their coalition with the African American community. The perceived initial need to defuse — with minimum visibility and vulnerability or the avoidance of agitation and publicity — racism and extreme nativism in America was now unnecessary or irksome. Somehow those primeval urges within the Jewish American community, which were the foundations of their coalition with the African American community, were now dissonant with their existential situation. On the one hand these foundations had been based on invoking the Talmudic prescriptions of constructive charity; acknowledging and acting upon an affinity for or identification with another group with a vaguely kindred past and a similarly persecuted present; accepting the idealistic promises and expectations of America; and assuming hegemonic responsibility for the management, financing, and administration — and the apparent triumph — of the civil rights movement.

On the other hand, the apparent lack of change in the objective character of the societal situation of the African American community, and its responses to it, urgently supported this need of the Jewish American community to reassess and redefine the goals, means, and priorities underlying its continued partnership in the coalition. For passionate hostility and bitter resentment were becoming, during the late 1960s and early 1970s, the most conspicuous characteristics of the special relationship between these two allies.

The complex meaning and interpretation of the Holocaust and the creation as well as the need for continued support of the state of Israel profoundly altered the consciousness, the goals, and the priorities of the Jewish American community.[4] At least two imperatives were learned from these two connecting events. First, from the Holocaust the Jewish American community came to realize that, however defined, the so-called civilized world was not to be trusted in the matter of world Jewry. Second, the Jewish American community — in spite of the contradiction of its being the exception to the general belief that Jewish communal life could not survive in the Diaspora — arrived at the conclusion that it was essential to secure a permanent, self-contained, sovereign place where all Jews, if necessary, could feel safe. Thus, the state of Israel and its well-being became an assurance that there would be no other Holocaust and that it would be always a sovereign refuge for all Jews.

The acceptance and legitimation of these imperatives, coinciding with the radical ideological changes transforming the African American community, profoundly altered the stance of the Jewish American community toward the defusing of racism in the United States, and thereby the nature of its coalition with the African American community. The Jewish American community could no longer define, sequentially, its relationship with the African American community as one based largely upon curiosity, empathy, and charity; then as a comradeship of the excluded; and eventually as a paternalistic concern and responsibility. The African American community had become transmuted; it was becoming a power group and would defer easily to no other interest group in America. The Jewish American community was faced with the harsh reality of the need to develop a new stance toward its ally — the African American community — and of establishing new relationships with the "strange" forces emanating from it.[5]

With this clear need for a shift in the goals of the coalition, from the perspective of the Jewish American community, went serious uncertainty about the apparent rejection by the African American community of customary strategies and tactics of the struggle for civil rights and the tolerance for or adoption of other disquieting strategies and tactics. There is reason to suspect that since the exploratory and discovery stage of the Jewish and African American alliance there had emerged a consensus about the appropriate or legitimate means for struggling for civil rights. Acceptable means of struggling included litigation, moral improvement, gentility and good manners, circumspect politics and ostentatious patriotism, educational achievement, and other self-help programs. The fragility of this consensus on legitimate means of struggling for civil rights was openly exposed by tensions in metropolitan areas during the 1930s, but the consensus literally fell apart during the late 1960s and early 1970s when the African American community tilted ideologically toward the endorsement of such strategies and survival techniques as armed resistance, terrorism and other forms of insurgency, demands for economic reparations, and advocacy of the principles of affirmative action.

The Jewish American community was caught in a cruel dilemma. The goals of becoming complete Americans and, at the same time, being fulfilled Jews (in the sense of guaranteeing throughout the world the continuity of a safe and vibrant Jewish communal life) and the reforming of the systemic racism of American society, in partnership with the African American community, had become displaced by a preemptive commitment to the development and ultimate security of the state of Israel.

The near consternation of the Jewish American community was compounded further by that fundamental contradiction created by the sanction of weapons of struggle used in the liberation and security of the state of Israel and disapproval and dismay at the use of some of the same weapons by the African American community. Johnson asserts, for instance, that the scientific use of violence and terror to break the will of liberal national rulers during the creation of the state of Israel was one of the superb Jewish contributions to the shape of the modern world.[6] Restitution and reparation for the atrocities of the Holocaust, and the support of the development of the state of Israel, were almost universally supported by the Jewish American community. But fear and dismay surrounded their applicability to the victims of the institution of slavery and, perhaps worse, to systemic racial segregation and discrimination in America.[7]

Thus, while the liberation movement[8] and the struggle to survive of the state of Israel and the civil rights struggles of the African American community are not precisely analogous, it may be argued tentatively that there were political and emotional similarities between Zionism and nationalistic ideologies indigenous to the African American community as contained in Pan-Africanism, the Garvey movement, and the so-called

Black Power movement. Unfortunately, however, it is not clear that there was widespread recognition of a possible affinity between these movements of liberation or sensitivity about their probable coalitional implications, within either the African or the Jewish American communities.

EXISTENTIAL POLITICS

One of the most destructive threats for the African and Jewish American alliance, rising in part out of the failure to understand the meaning of the intrinsic universal character of almost all liberation movements, became the perceived antagonism of the emerging so-called Black Power movement to the traditional pattern of coalition formation within the pluralistic context of American society. This seemed especially so between two such minority groups as the African and Jewish American communities. The fact of race itself had come to be seen as a limit to coalition, and this state of affairs of the alliance evolved out of the civil rights movement in the changing context of American society.

A curious feature of the civil rights movement, at its zenith between approximately 1954 and 1965, stands out when compared with quick or rapid social change then taking place in other nations. This feature is that objective change in the racist system of America apparently was being driven or induced by the combination of a strategy and philosophy — passive or nonviolent resistance — involving the principled suffering of those who had already suffered most, rather than through an approach involving naked and ruinous violence. A consequence of this curious feature of induced social change for the African American community was the possibility that if objective change did not approximate the expected reality or redress appreciably longtime and persisting grievances, there was the appalling risk of extinguishing collective hope, and if hope were extinguished, desperation would be created. Moreover, as we have seen, the civil rights movement up to now tended to result largely in symbolic rather than substantive change in the status of the African American community.

Out of this existential situation — for by approximately 1965 the objective situation of the African American community had reached what can be described only as that of profound alienation and discontent — emerged a primeval sense of the power of dying, of running the risk of personal jeopardy and making the commitment to go to jail and remain there and of recruiting others to do the same. The emergence of the Black Power movement — and one of its variants, the Black Panther

Party — out of the civil rights movement, then, was nourished by the growing realization by at least a significant segment of the African American community of this ultimate sense of the need for social power. Black Power then meant anything, including violence, that contributed to the self-determination of African Americans, anything that placed them in such a position that it would be too expensive nationally for the African American community to continue to be dehumanized and exploited. As will be seen later, the emergence and legitimation of this ideology of Black Power contributed importantly to divisive strains dormant within both the African American community and the African and Jewish American alliance.

Much has been written about the ideology of the Black Power movement: its philosophy, ethics, strategies, and conceptions of the self-identity of African Americans.[9] Therefore, before addressing our chief concern, which is to examine some implications of the emergence between 1965 and 1979 of this ideology upon the Jewish and African American alliance, some attention must be given to the Black Power movement itself.

The Black Power movement differed in two significant ways from the traditional civil rights movement as managed largely by the NAACP, the Urban League, and the African and Jewish American alliance. Its thrust was aimed both at what may be called loosely the WASP structure of dominating power and control in general as well as in particular the apparent complicity of the African and Jewish American alliance in the maintenance of that racist system inextricably interwoven into the structure of dominance in America. In other words, the intent of the Black Power movement was almost nihilistic: to undermine the existing social order in America with little or no emphasis placed upon laying out a new social order.

The other difference was what may be called the Black Power movement's tone. It exhibited an apparent lack of restraint about the sensibilities of the dominant WASP majority in America, those of the Jewish American community, or those of the traditional African American leadership and intellectual elites. Its explicit purpose, rather, was to capture the support of the African American masses and to refrain from giving understanding or insight to the dominant WASP majority. This difference, moreover, tended to legitimate the insouciant and militant activism that was a conspicuous characteristic of the Black Power movement.

Within these two major differences between the Black Power movement and the traditional civil rights movement were masked significant corollary themes. With respect to the former difference, the Black Power movement carried within it a serious critique of the capitalistic system of the nation.[10] With respect to the latter difference, involving the African and Jewish American alliance (and including WASP liberals), the Black Power movement seemed intent upon rejecting the value of integration or assimilation and substituting for it the doctrine of Black Separatism.[11] Capturing the political allegiance of, or obtaining dominance over, the African American community became the prime target of the Black Power movement and thereby, ipso facto, contributed to the development of its cultural and political autonomy or racial self-determination.

Another not insignificant difference between the Black Power movement and the traditional civil rights movement was its shift in locus. Before this period of 1965–1979 the violence and recalcitrancy of the southern region of the United States in matters of race relations had tended to make it the most prominent battleground of the civil rights struggle. Parenthetically, this reality of place for the civil rights struggle had been — since early in the coalition formation process of the African and Jewish American alliance — a constant source of discord within the Jewish American community. For the southern component of the Jewish American community had tended consistently to register grave reservations about the prominence of the Jewish American community in the civil rights struggle and, as well, the entire alliance or coalition with the African American community.[12]

Now, however, to this southern arena were joined with vehemence the excruciating problems of the African American masses concentrated in the urban and metropolitan areas dispersed throughout the nation.[13] The specters of Malcolm X, H. "Rap" Brown, Eldridge Cleaver, Stokely Carmichael, and Fred Hampton now arose to trouble both the WASP power structure and the African and Jewish American alliance.

This dispersal and expansion of the "strange" new confrontational activities of the civil rights and the Black Power movements could not help but contribute to the ensuing internal strife, dissension, and factional conflict within all segments of the civil rights struggle. It is not difficult to understand how, ultimately, such internal tensions and strains converged to contribute to what may be described as a period of organizational chaos among the voluntary associations and agencies involved in the struggle for civil rights.

Simultaneous with the shift (described above) of the civil rights struggle from essentially a southern region to a national level during the 1960s, there emerged a bitter racial and ideological conflict over the participatory roles of European and Jewish Americans in the major organizations (especially CORE and SNCC) conducting the civil rights struggle. It would seem that the mere fact of race itself had become a prime limit to coalition.[14] The consequences of this conflict contributed greatly to the developing schism within the African and Jewish American alliance.

A predilection by the Black Power movement toward favoring the cultivation of ties or connections by the African American community with Third World nations, in opposition to the traditional tactical pattern of forging alliances with "WASP and other liberal interests" in the United States, is another difference between the established, mainstream civil rights movement and the Black Power movement. This difference was a piece of the transformation of the ideological roots of the civil rights struggle — customarily grounded in pacifism, legalism, and religious radicalism — into an international perspective based upon secular notions of race, class, and formally anti-Western imperialism and anticapitalism. This transformation, largely under the initiative of SNCC, was revealed in the early resistance to American involvement in Vietnam, trips to Third World nations, public expressions of solidarity with foreign radical and revolutionary groups, the tilting toward the adoption of Pan-Africanist or Marxian doctrines, and publicly taking a pro-Palestinian position, thereby interpreted as an anti-Jewish or an anti-Israeli stand in the politics of the Middle East.[15]

The presence of international roots in the historic civil rights struggle was not new. At least as early as the life and works of Edward W. Blyden,[16] the scholarship and activism of W. E. B. Dubois, and the programs of Marcus M. Garvey, and during the revolutionary career of Antonio Maceo in Cuba[17] the civil rights struggle of the African American community has been more than merely touched by the ferment of international liberation movements. What is novel during this 1965–1979 period, however, is the coinciding of this ideological transformation, borne by the Black Power movement, with the dismantling of Western European imperialism and colonialism and the emergence on the world scene of what are called Third World nations. This yoking of what heretofore had been considered a domestic issue with international policy and practice was devastating to the solidarity of the African and Jewish American alliance, disruptive of a kind of understood unity with other segments of the civil rights movement, and potentially troublesome for the federal government.

The perspective of the Black Power movement, in other words, was quite unlike that held by the African and Jewish American alliance, the latter being generally perceived, at this time, as the vanguard of the civil rights movement. As a social movement the Black Power movement operated on the basic premise that incisive change in the system of race relations in America would emerge only out of the cultural, political, economic, and psychological mobilization of the African American community.

It advocated a strategy of militant activism and tended to deemphasize the norm or value of nonviolence; held serious reservations about the goal of integration and interracial democracy; supported a serious critique of industrial capitalism; and attempted to disengage from established or entrenched ties with allies (purportedly to rupture the traditional patterns of dependency of the African American community) and supported the forging of new alliances with international and domestic allies. Moreover, the Black Power movement tended to be indifferent to possible threats of repression and the losses of financial and other types of support. All in all, the Black Power movement was perceived, both by the African and Jewish American alliance and the federal government, with dismay and fear.

Coincidental with the zenith of the above ideological clash within the civil rights struggle was the appearance of mass upheavals in the urban and metropolitan areas of the nation that seriously could be taken to be preliminaries to insurrection, rebellion, or revolution. Between approximately 1964 and 1969 there were hundreds of conflicts between African Americans and, largely, the local law enforcement agencies of their communities.[18] These mass protests or uprisings were of a different order of reality from the activities of the civil rights and Black Power movements.[19] While essentially urban mass disturbances, they tended to involve the destruction and expropriation of property, a reckless endangerment of life, and defiance of civil authorities and were responded to with ruthless reprisals by local, state, and federal law enforcement agencies in the form of indiscriminate arrests, general harassment, brutality, and violent deaths. Generally considered to be unorganized, the only purposes that have been attributed consistently to these urban disorders are symbolic — that is, the seeking of the end of racist exploitation and dehumanization in the neighborhoods of African Americans and the privilege or right of African Americans to control their own fates.[20]

Violence was unusually blatant throughout most of the 1960 decade as demonstrated by the assassinations of Medgar Evers, John F. Kennedy, Malcolm X, Martin L. King, Jr., and Robert Kennedy and, as well, by the responses to young Americans protesting continued national involvement in the Vietnam War. In September 1963, the Sixteenth Street

Baptist Church in Birmingham, Alabama, was bombed, and four young girls — Carole Robertson, Cynthia Wesley, Denise McNair, and Addie Mae Collins — were killed and at least 20 others were injured.[21] On Sunday, June 21, 1964, three civil rights workers, an interracial team — James Chaney, Andrew Goodman, and Michael Schwerner — disappeared and were subsequently murdered in or about Philadelphia, Mississippi.[22] These selected instances of violence, it should be noted, were in no way instigated by or directly connected with the Black Power movement.

There is little doubt that the solidarity of the African and Jewish American alliance was severely strained by this ambience of violence and the spontaneous urban disorders throughout the nation during the middle and the end of the 1960s. But even more devastating to the coalition were the issues surfacing near the end of the decade and continuing during most of the 1970s out of the drive for community control in the national educational reform movement and the implementation of school desegregation embodied in the policy of affirmative action or, as its opponents labeled it, reverse discrimination.

The controversies surrounding the issue of community control, and especially those involving the nexus of relationships between the African and Jewish American communities, are most clearly seen in the 1966 Mount Vernon, New York, clash over school segregation between African and Jewish Americans[23] and in the 1968 United Federation of Teachers strike in New York City against the Ocean Hill-Brownsville school district involving labor (the entitlement of teachers and principals) and public policy issues such as school desegregation, decentralization, and community control.[24]

In these controversies the clashing interests with which the Jewish and African American alliance had to contend are revealed openly. These interests tended to be articulated in symbolic catch words or slogans such as "community control," "affirmative action," "quotas," "nationalism," "gradualism," "anti-Semitism," "racism," "separatism," "preferential treatment," and "reverse discrimination." Moreover, the venom with which these terms ordinarily were used in disputation and throughout coverage by the mass media threatened vitally the tendency toward the norm of consensus politics commonly found heretofore in the texture of interaction within the African and Jewish American alliance.

At issue, fundamentally, in these skirmishes over the schooling system was the direction of the shifting politics of racism. The massive thrust of the Black Power movement from within the African American community (as located jointly in its working and lower classes, the cohort of college youths, and the idealistic and/or disgruntled middle classes with unfullfilled expectations) was for equality and justice now. The advocacy of this position is best exemplified by the epic heroism — the apparent belief that the substance of educational excellency and educational equality is almost always a matter of endeavor and hence a matter of calculated activism — of Rhody McCoy, administrator of the Ocean Hill-Brownsville school district. This thrust was counterposed against that emphasis of the Jewish American community (as located particularly in its middle class strata) on "individual merit" as the penultimate basis for advancement, recognition, and achievement. The advocacy of this position is best exemplified by the trenchant leadership of Albert Shanker, president of the United Federation of Teachers union.

This bitter conflict involved, at another level, an intractable dispute over the very nature of the systems of preferment, or ways of distributing rewards, in institutionalized bureaucratic structures (for example, the schooling system) and the often nationalistic demands for special consideration — for an equal share in all of society now — through special entitlements and changes of the customary rules of systemic governance. Regardless of analytic level, friction became so intense between the African and Jewish American communities at this time that it attracted international attention.

The divisiveness of the African and Jewish American alliance peaked during the early and mid-1970s over the implementation of the principle of affirmative action, especially in the public sectors of American society, with the saga of Allan Bakke.[25] The tendency toward consensus characteristic of earlier campaigns in the civil rights struggle had dissipated. The African and Jewish American alliance was literally decimated, for Jewish American community organizations were, shockingly, allied with other European American ethnic, police, and conservative groups in offering briefs opposing affirmative action implementation on the basis of preferential treatment, reverse discrimination, and quotas. The Bakke saga may be described as the nadir of the African and Jewish American alliance.

The evidence and the argument of this chapter suggest that, between 1965 and 1979, as a result of a cumulative process of divergence in perceptions about their existential situation, a schism of such severity emerged within the African and Jewish American alliance as to threaten the continuity of the coalition. The roots of this schism appear to be such substantial change in the definitions of goals, practices, and priorities as to negate, except symbolically, the essential preconditions of a visible coalition.[26]

First, there clearly was some indication of nonrecognition of, or insensitivity to, the respective self-interests of the African and Jewish American communities: on the one hand the drive for self-determination, liberation, and redress for historic wrongs on the part of the African American community, on the other hand the clear commitment to the development and ultimate security of the state of Israel by the Jewish American community. Second, few grounds existed for continuing to believe that mutual benefit for each party stemmed from their coalition or alliance. In fact, much tended to be made of the reciprocal exploitations — for example, financial assistance, intellectual, administrative and managerial domination, and the psychic rewards and costs of the role sets of interpreter, broker, and champion that contributed to the moral obligation of collective dependency — that allegedly made up a large part of their customary collaboration. Third, there was difficulty in accepting the fact, and this seemed to have been especially painful for the Jewish American community, that each party to the coalition had its own independent base of power and should not be dependent for policy determination upon an external force. Thus was legitimated the knowledge acquired through experience in the American context that race itself could be construed as a limit to long-term or permanent coalition. And, finally, there was difficulty — especially on the part of the African American community — in realizing that concrete and specific, as opposed to general and idealistic, goals should be the fundamental objectives of any coalition.

Five or six key events or issues may be abstracted selectively from the multiplicity of activities in the civil rights struggle during the 1960s and 1970s to highlight that disintegrative process that brought the alliance or coalition of the African and Jewish American communities to this fateful juncture of imminent collapse. In June 1964, and as a part of the pervasive escalation in that so American tradition of violence, there was the disappearance and subsequent murder of three civil rights workers — two were Jewish Americans and one was an African American — in or about Philadelphia, Mississippi.

Then there was the organizational disarray among the factions of the civil rights movement within the African American community. This is exemplified most dramatically by two episodic events or ongoing activities: the efforts between approximately 1964 and 1967 to expel European and Jewish Americans from, or redefine drastically their participatory roles in, leadership positions of the liberation struggle of African Americans and the national prominence given, in early 1967, to the organization and activism of the Black Panther Party under the leadership of Huey Newton, Bobby Seale, and Eldridge Cleaver. Insult was added to injury by the public announcement later in that year of a formal alliance between SNCC and the Black Panther Party.

One of the most devastating events to contribute to the instability of the coalition, following the Six-Day's War victory of the state of Israel over Arab forces, was the publication of statements by SNCC in July 1967 supporting the Palestinian position in the Arab-Israel conflict in the Middle East. The smoldering tensions cannot be overlooked, either, that arose over the issues of community control, charges of anti-Semitism, and charges of racism surrounding the implementation of public school desegregation and bureaucratic decentralization in New York City, culminating in the 1968 American Federation of Teachers' union strike during the Ocean Hill-Brownsville school district controversy.

Finally, there was the turmoil about the issue of affirmative action and "quotas" — the code word for opposition to policies and practices designed to open areas of education and employment where African Americans and other minorities traditionally had been excluded — ending with the 1978 Supreme Court decision in the case of the *Regents of the University of California* v. *Bakke*. These key events are emblematic of those disintegrative forces marking the strategic disagreements between the African and Jewish American communities as embodied in their alliance or coalition, which culminated in the most drastic breach of their special relationship. The severity of this disorganized stage of the process of alliance by the end of the 1970s was to flow over into the civil rights struggles of the 1980s.

NOTES

1. The nature of the racial desegregation process and its results in these institutional areas of American society are described in some detail in the following works: Nalty, *Strength for the Fight*; Arthur R. Ashe, Jr., *A Hard Road to Glory: The Roots of Sports in America* (New York: Warner Books, 1988); Southern, *Music of Black Americans*; Derrick Bell, *And We Are Not Saved: The Elusive Quest for Racial Justice* (New York: Basic Books, Inc., 1979); and Betsy Levin and Willis D. Hawley, eds., "School Desegregation: Lessons on the First Twenty-Five Years," *Law and Contemporary Problems* 42:1 & 2 (Summer/Autumn 1978).

2. For a detailed discussion of the emergence and evolution of this foreign policy see Harry S. Ashmore, "Containment, Confrontation, Detente," *The Center Magazine* VII:1 (January/February 1974): 40–48.

3. Johnson, *History of the Jews,* pp. 566–68. By this time, according to Johnson, the Jewish American minority's "aristocracy of success became as ubiquitous and pervasive in its cultural influence as the earlier elite, the White Anglo-Saxon

Protestant." And, politically, Johnson claims that "of all the great American votes, the Jewish vote was the best organized, the most responsive to guidance by its leaders and the most likely to exert itself effectively."

4. Ibid., Parts 6 and 7. An excellent view of the complexity of this process of altering the consciousness, goals, and priorities of the Jewish American community is provided by Harvey Molotch, "American Jews and the State of Israel," *The Center Magazine* XVI:3 (May/June 1983): 8–26. Also see Hertzberg, *The Jews in America,* (New York: Simon and Schuster, 1989), Chapters 19 and 20.

5. Hertzberg, *The Jews in America,* pp. 348–49.

6. Johnson, *History of the Jews,* p. 521.

7. Ibid., pp. 513–17 for details of the meanness and arrogance associated with attempts to secure moral as well as financial compensation for the Holocaust. I find it curious, too, that historically the United States has made reparations and restitution, without unusual rancor, to Native Americans, Eskimos, Hawaiians, and some Asian Americans but made no such redress in the instance of the unique situation of the progeny of African slaves.

8. Here I use what was essentially the first anticolonial struggle, largely of European Jewry against the British Empire, following World War II as a war of national liberation. See Johnson, *History of the Jews,* pp. 520–28.

9. The following sources have been especially helpful in preparing this section about the Black Power movement: Geschwender, *The Black Revolt,* Part III; Garrow, *Bearing the Cross,* Chapter 9; Stokely Carmichael & Charles V. Hamilton, *Black Power: The Politics of Liberation in America* (New York: Vintage Books, 1967); Carson, *In Struggle,* Chapters 13 and 14; and Blumberg, *Civil Rights,* Chapter 8. To get a sense of the rhetoric as well as the substance of the descriptions and accounts of Black Power during this particular period I urge the sampling of the works of, among others, Clayton Riley, W. H. Ferry, James Boggs, Addison Gayle, Jr., Yahne Sangare, Richard Gibson, Robert Staples, and Richard A. Long to be found in Volumes 7–10 of the *Liberator* magazine. Also worthy of note for their treatment of the phenomenon of the Black Power movement are selected essays and articles to be found in Volumes 1–5 (1967–1974) of *The Black Scholar.*

10. See Raymond S. Franklin, "The Political Economy of Black Power," in Geschwender, *The Black Revolt,* pp. 224–30.

11. See Carson, *In Struggle,* Chapter 13; Blumberg, *Civil Rights,* pp. 129–31. A definitive treatment of the doctrine of Black separatism, especially from an African American perspective, is to be found in Raymond L. Hall, ed., *Black Separatism and Social Reality: Rhetoric and Reason* (New York: Pergamon Press, Inc., 1977).

12. Hertzberg, *The Jews in America,* pp. 335–36.

13. Franklin, *Political Economy of Black Power,* pp. 222–24; Blumberg, *Civil Rights,* pp. 136–37.

14. For an intimate and detailed treatment of the process, as well as the personal and organizational havoc of this conflict, see Meier and Rudwick, *CORE: A Study in the Civil Rights Movement 1942–1968* (Urbana: University of Illinois Press, 1975), pp. 379–93, 412–25. Also, see Carson, *In Struggle,* pp. 196–206, 236–42.

15. See Carson, *In Struggle,* pp. 265–86. The background of that famous episode involving the preparation of a paper by SNCC supporting the Arab position in the Middle East conflict, following the Six-Day's War in June 1967 and an account of the

retaliatory, sustained attack on the organization by the Jewish American community is presented on pp. 266–69.

16. Lynch, *Edward Wilmot Blyden*.

17. W. M. Phillips, Jr., "Race Relations in Cuba: Some Reflections," *The Review of Black Political Economy* 8:2 (Winter 1978): 175.

18. Otto Kerner, *Report of the National Advisory Commission on Civil Disorders* (New York: The New York Times Co., 1968). See Chapter 1 for a summary of what actually happened.

19. Geschwender, *The Black Revolt*, Part IV. See also Blumberg, *Civil Rights*, Chapter 9.

20. Geschwender, *The Black Revolt*, p. 253. The causes of and who participated in these urban disorders have yet to be answered conclusively by studies from either the deprivation and relative deprivation, the resource mobilization, or the collective action theories of social movements. See Karl-Dieter Opp, "Grievances and Participation in Social Movements," *American Sociological Review* 53:6 (December 1988): 853–64. The most plausible explanation, or insightful understanding, of these mass behaviors I have found is located in Albert Murray, *The Omni-Americans: New Perspectives on Black Experience and American Culture* (New York: Outerbridge & Dienstfrey, 1970), Chapter 1.

21. Garrow, *Bearing the Cross*, p. 294.

22. Ibid., p. 342.

23. Robert Weisbrot, *Freedom Bound: A History of America's Civil Rights Movement* (New York: W. W. Norton, 1990), p. 242.

24. Maurice R. Berube and Marilyn Gittell, eds., *Confrontation at Ocean Hill-Brownsville* (New York: Frederick A. Praeger, 1969); Alphonso Pinkney, "Recent Unrest Between Blacks and Jews: The Claims of Anti-Semitism and Reverse Discrimination," *The Black Sociologist* 8 (Fall-Summer 1978/79): 44–51; and Kaufman, *Broken Alliance*, pp. 139–64.

25. Tollett, "What Led to Bakke," pp. 2–10; Pinkney, "Recent Unrest Between Blacks and Jews," pp. 51–54; Eric Foner, "Point of View," *The Chronicle of Higher Education* (March 13, 1978); J. Harvie Wilkinson III, *From Brown to Bakke* (New York: Oxford, 1979), see especially Chapters 10 and 11 and the epilogue.

26. Carmichael and Hamilton, *Black Power*, pp. 79–80.

7

The 1980s

Andrew Young resigned as U.S. Ambassador to the United Nations Organization on August 15, 1979. This action was prompted, apparently, by a leak into the public domain about an unauthorized or clandestine meeting he had held with representatives of the PLO, such meetings violating allegedly understood, and secret, agreements between at least official representatives of the governments of the state of Israel and the United States. An appointee of President Jimmy Carter, Young had come to be considered in some circles — largely because of the refreshing, trusting, and unusually favorable relations established with many of the so-called Third World nations — a political liability for the Democratic Party in the approaching presidential reelection campaign.

The African American community, in almost all of its aspects, was enraged. It uniformly and openly accused the Jewish American community, in collusion with the state of Israel, of instigating the Young resignation. The charge was denied vehemently by the Jewish American community.

As an immediate aftermath of this nationally and internationally publicized event the already uneasy coalition between the Jewish and African American communities seemed to collapse into shambles. This present disintegrative tendency within the coalition had been preceded somewhat earlier in the 1970s by some slight measure of reconciliation following the upsurge of tensions apparently generated by the New York City school desegregation and decentralization crisis in the late 1960s and the early 1970s. As has been seen, a most virulent period of anger, bitterness, and even hatred then followed; and now this was to be repeated. The quality of the relations between these two minority communities, and their concerted actions, throughout the 1980s was to be dominated again by recrimination, anger, bitterness, and, possibly, even hatred.[1]

This historic phase of the African and Jewish American alliance features rancorous strife, confrontation, and competition heretofore unseen between the two minority communities. A fire storm of charges and countercharges were raised in numerous meetings and conferences throughout the nation in the attempt to resolve this apparent rupture of the coalition. Four major charges, on an objective level, were made against the African American community. First, it was accused of being sympathetic, in general, to that perception of the state of Israel as essentially a symbol of colonialism, racism, and imperialism. Second, significant segments of the African American community were accused of being favorable to a position supportive of the Arabs and PLO in the turmoil of the Middle East conflicts and, thereby, were perceived to be fundamentally hostile to that penultimate goal of the Jewish American community of assuring the security of the state of Israel. Third, anti-Semitism was said to be rampant throughout the African American community. And, finally, there was the emergence of the so-called "Jesse Jackson factor" during the two presidential election campaigns of the decade.

Counteracting these charges, on the objective level, five major charges were raised against the Jewish American community. While conceding past support of and cooperation with the African American community it was accused, first, of being insensitive in general to issues held to be of crucial importance to the African American com-munity. Second, the Jewish American community was condemned for its almost unified position of opposition to the principle of affirmative action. Third, it was charged with complicity in the destruction of a cherished symbol by conspiring to force the resignation of Ambassador Young. Fourth, it was held to be compliant with and supportive of the alleged ties between the state of Israel and the Republic of South Africa — the latter perceived to be the world's paragon of racism, tyranny, and social injustice and a blatant violator of human rights. And, finally, the Jewish American community was censured for the arrogant, moralistic, and patronizing tones in which its admonitions and criticisms of the African American community were couched.

The patent simplicity of these charges and countercharges for understanding the troubles of the African and Jewish American alliance — almost 90 years of coalitional solidarity and consensus — seem unreal, given the particular historical moment and the specific political situation. Early in the 1980s the Carter administration was replaced by the Reagan administration. It is uncontestable that this transfer of control of the federal government from the Democrats to the Republicans ushered in a definite change in the character of public policy. This vital change involved the emerging domination in public policy of an essentially conservative, if not reactionary, perspective of the role of the federal government in civil rights matters, and it placed the previous essentially liberal perspective — both within the governmental system as well as throughout the nation — in a defensive posture. This change in the character of public policy meant that, pragmatically, issues traditionally of paramount concern to the African and Jewish American coalition — such as, among others, access to higher education, open housing, affirmative action, prison reform, the right to vote, court-ordered school busing, job training and employment-related programs, and support of the welfare system and poverty-oriented programs — were severely deemphasized.

Precisely at this time, too, serious attention began to be paid to that classic sociological question of how societies allocate scarce resources and benefits. In this instance, convincing evidence was amassed that showed the increasing concentration of wretched poverty in urban African American residential areas. Associated with this development was the public issue of the emergence of the so-called underclass as a permanent class formation in America as well as in other advanced industrial societies generally.[2]

Adventures in military aggression were undertaken by the nation, essentially unilaterally, in Central America, the Caribbean, North Africa, the Middle East, and in the Persian Gulf. Contests for power between the executive and legislative branches of the federal government intensified, especially in the foreign policy domain, and fall-out from these contests contributed ultimately to the Iran/Contra saga of alleged misguided patriotism, personal as well as bureaucratic corruption, and systemic anomie.

Three international developments during the 1980s must be mentioned in order to help establish the particularity of this historical and political period for the African and Jewish American alliance. First, there was the tremendous rise in importance throughout the world of what has been called transnational social phenomena.[3] This is attributed partly to ecological and climatological changes of some magnitude but, more importantly, to the dramatic globalization of networks of all kind that took place throughout the decade. These global linkages are imputed to be the essential core of transnational social phenomena. They are said to "range from international banking, trade and market networks, economic and military interdependencies, labor and political migrations, international standards and regulation, intellectual and information exchanges, multi-lateral treaties, multinational corporations, and energy and technology flows, to religious missionary movements, advertising media, and the cosmopolitanization of a middle-class consumer culture·"4 In myriad ways the mutual as well as disparate interests of both the African and Jewish American communities were vitally touched by the emergence of this globalization of informational networks or transnational social phenomena.

There was, second, the firm entrenchment of Japan, as well as other nations of the Pacific Rim, into superpower status. It is too early to assess the full implications of this development, but there is little doubt that it has had tremendous impacts upon both domestic and international policies and practices of the United States. Moreover, divergent interpretations of these policies and practices of trade, sanctions, loans, cultural exchanges, military and nonmilitary compacts and interventions, and so forth, easily can be seen to have direct and indirect consequences for the self-serving interests of both the African and Jewish American communities.

Finally, there was the intensification of that paradox of Americanization, on the international level, involving the perceptual divorce of the U.S. government from that of the American culture. That is, the continued, if not intensified, of that profoundly anti-American stance of major parts of the non-European or non-Western world, while, at the same time, the elite behaviors, popular sentiments, leisure, and life styles of these same nations were so deeply influenced by American cultural models. Many of the deliberations and actions of the United Nations demonstrate, at first hand, the reality of this paradox. The status of the American government as a superpower, and especially in the implementation of its foreign policy, was most profoundly affected during the 1980s by this paradox of Americanization. Thus, the disintegrative tendencies of the African and Jewish American alliance peaked during a particular historical period characterized, at least in broad perspective, by the confounding influences of these three specific geopolitical, economic, and psychological realities.

This quick look at the contextual background of the 1980s was essential for any attempt to understand or explain the cruel predicament facing the African and Jewish American alliance. Perhaps there are available more fundamental factors than anti-Semitism allegedly endemic within the African American community, mutual intergroup insensitivity, the tradition of leadership dominance by the Jewish American community in the policy determination phases of the civil rights struggle, the patronizing arrogance — as well as the existential reality of an elastic or indeterminate standard of moral, ethical, and racial judgment within the coalitional politics of race — directed by the Jewish American community toward the African American community, and the attempt to remove from major consideration the impotence of the African American community in matters of American foreign policy (especially when compared with the instances of the Polish American community and the Solidarity movement or the Jewish American community and the state of Israel). These factors, and perhaps more, at least help in gaining appreciation of the contextual background for the bitter estrangement during most of the 1980s within the historic coalition between the African and Jewish American communities.

SHIFTING FROM CONFRONTATION TO POLITICS

Out of the bitter disappointments over the decades since the 1954 U.S. Supreme Court *Brown* decision and the "all deliberate speed" formula of the 1955 *Brown II* decision, the African American community had learned a fundamental truth. It was that while the issues of rights and justices in the civil rights struggle were necessary, they were not sufficient or essential for inducing appreciable and timely change in the racist system of America. In other words, the placing of emphasis largely upon justice and rights in the civil rights struggle — the dilemma of morality — served often to obscure the at least equally vital issues of power, domination, and control.[5]

Thus, during the 1980s the pursuit of social power within American society became, ostensibly, the paramount goal of the African American community. With the acquisition of social power in America, in justifying this objective, the timely attainment of equity of minority group status as well as collective justice for the African American community became possible. In short, and extending an observation of Charles S. Johnson,[6] no longer were the church, the lodge, the Greek-letter fraternities and sororities, and the civil rights organizations to absorb the potential political energies of African Americans.

But the pursuit of social power, that is, legitimating the goal of sharing directly rather than as a client or pawn in the domains of dominance and control in America, presented at least two serious risks. The first of these was the possibility of fatally damaging the core of solidarity or the organizational integration — the bedrock consensus — of the African American community over that existential matter of its collective fate in American society.

The second risk, and that which is of most pressing concern here, was that of the continued integrity of that long-standing alliance between the African and Jewish American communities. For clearly, and in the most gross terms, such a shift in group objective could transform the relations of the African and Jewish American communities as minority groups in a predominately WASP society from the historic coalitional mode into a directly competitive one.

Several developments are at hand to suggest that, indeed, a pragmatic shift from confrontation to politics did occur within the African American community during the 1980s. Examining these developments should offer some insight into why this shift from confrontation to politics happened and permit inferences about its meanings for the historic African and Jewish American alliance.

After the 1980–1981 recession, when there was a panic-like national response because European American unemployment rose to double-digit figures comparable to that commonly considered normal for African Americans, the contextual situation for the African American community was fundamentally altered by the replacement of the Carter with the Reagan administration. This transfer of power in the federal government represented more than a mere symbolic change from a Democratic to a Republican party regime. From the perspective of the interests of the African American community it was a crucial reorientation from what reasonably may be called a liberal to a conservative political philosophy.

We are now too close, and it is much too early, to assess objectively the impact upon the African and Jewish American alliance and the entire civil rights struggle of the Reagan administration. It is irrefutable, however, that a principal element of the conservative political orientation of that administration was to deemphasize, or even to attempt to halt, those special entitlement programs intended to increase the hiring and promotion of African Americans, women, and other minorities who had been discriminated against in the past. Also, it is clear that there was to be a reduced emphasis on human rights as a basis for U.S. foreign policy. The reasoning of the conservatives, apparently, was that now it was safe to dismantle the social welfare programs and the civil rights agencies attempting to provide relief against poverty and racism without the African American community and its allies reacting violently as oppressed peoples have reacted elsewhere throughout the world. The African American community, in other words, apparently was defined by the Reagan administration as being essentially powerless, or it was perceived to be entrenched in the confusions of a false consciousness.

However, there was a development successfully brought off during the Reagan administration that held devastating implications for the African and Jewish American alliance. This was the broadening by the federal government of the concept "minority" to include other minorities and women. In other words, distinction was no longer to be made by the federal government between racial and other customary forms of collective oppression and dehumanization such as, for example, religion, gender, ethnic, and sexual orientation or preference.

It merits noting here that the original and steadfast intent of the African American community, throughout the long history of the civil rights struggle, was a moral and constitutional campaign against racial indignities, inequities, and injustices. Now, with definition, corruption of perception, and subtle rationalization, the grievances of other disadvantaged or oppressed groups in the nation were to be piggy-backed upon that of the plight of the African American community.

The immediate consequence of the completion of this metamorphosis of the concept minority during the 1980s was that, again, a deadly price was to be exacted from the African American community for being in the vanguard of the civil and human rights struggle; it had always carried historically the main physical, emotional, moral, and psychological burden of this national injustice. That dream of sharing the privileges and rights of justice, freedom, and equality of the African American community was being pressed further into the anonymity of the collective consciousness of the members of American society.

A second development complicating the shift from confrontation to politics during the 1980s was the emergence within the Jewish American community of the perception of the African American community as a definite electoral threat within the internal political life of the United States dominated by vocal self-interest or special interest groups. The African American community generally, by this time, had become pivotal in local, state, and to some extent national politics. Its members had become more skillful in exploiting the American system of open politics, and apparently were gradually renouncing their historic indirect or subservient pattern of so-called clientage politics. For example, in the 20 years since the first African American mayor was elected there had been elected over 300 African Americans to that office in cities ranging from Gary (Indiana), Los Angeles, Newark (New Jersey), Atlanta, New Orleans, and Detroit to Tuskegee (Alabama). The African American community could no longer safely be perceived by the Jewish American community as politically quiescent and ineffective.

At least three factors seem important to a minority group in establishing effective influence in the American political process — establishing an electoral threat, developing a lobbying apparatus, and demonstrating consonance with the symbols of American nationhood. The African American community had become politically credible by the 1980s (some four or five decades after its ally, the Jewish American community, had reached this approximate stature). It had convinced the dominant political parties that a substantial number of African Americans could be persuaded to vote according to their beliefs and interests on election day. Moreover, there was some indication that the African American community could be induced to shift loyalties from one party to the other and, as well, would shift loyalties from one candidate to another within the same party.

Potentially, then, the African American community had become an electoral threat, and especially so to the Jewish American community. The tensions created in the Jewish American community during the 1980s by the so-called Jesse Jackson factor become more intelligible in terms of the African American community being perceived as a potential electoral threat. A significant example was the charisma of Jesse Jackson as a presidential candidate — the organizational astuteness of his campaign as well as its apparent reception by the American public. The emergent potentiality for lobbying in the unique interests of the African American community inherent in the Jesse Jackson factor was not lost upon the Jewish American community.

The keystone of an effective lobbying apparatus in the political process is organization. Several factors contributed to the building of an incipient lobby for the African American community. Superimposed upon that traditional community organization foundation of churches, historically predominately African American colleges and universities, fraternal and service organizations, and the civil rights organizations was, first, the legitimation of Jesse Jackson as a politician of national stature. Second, an issue came into prominent view that most of the citizens of the United States as well as the nations of the world could support: the infamy of the system of apartheid of the Republic of South Africa, the addressing of which could test and prove the emergent organizational apparatus. Third, there was the maturing of the so-called Black Caucus in the U.S. Congress. This entity represented a unifying ideological center of elected African American officials at the national level and involved networking ties with politicians (African Americans and others) at the state and local and even international levels.

One significant fact must be noted here, because, in my opinion, it illustrates the complexity and perhaps even resilience of the historic African and Jewish American alliance. Throughout all of the sweep of disintegrative forces during the 1960s and 1970s creating turmoil within the coalition of the African and Jewish American communities one linkage remained essentially steadfast. This was that compact apparently held between Jewish and African American elected members of Congress. As strange as it may seem, the Black Caucus consistently supported aid packages designed for the state of Israel. In return, Jewish American members of Congress consistently supported social programs designed to help the disadvantaged and to correct systemic injustice.

Several changes finally took place that appeared to converge so as to heighten African American political consciousness and astuteness. They were: changes in the structures of opportunity for African Americans (especially in education, employment, political enfranchisement, and the military establishment), alterations through the processes of social mobility in the class structure of the African American community, and the tempering of the identity and solidarity of the African American community as derived — directly and indirectly — from the activities of the 1960s and 1970s civil rights and Black Power movements.

Thus, another link in the establishment of political influence of the African American community was forged. The Jewish American community — accustomed as it was to playing traditionally an interpreter and champion role toward the political and cultural interests of its historic ally — could not but interpret with grave misgivings the meaning of these developments toward the independent pursuit of social power by the African American community.

The third essential requirement of the African American community for achieving effective influence in the American political process involved establishing constancy with and celebrating, along with other Americans, the supremacy of the American way of life. This has been extremely difficult for the African American community to do, largely because of the existence and intractability of the racist system. Yet, historically, severe criticisms of the African American community have been made precisely because, overwhelmingly and consistently, it has always shown a cultural perspective and philosophy essentially identical with that desired and expected by the WASP majority. Sometimes, even derisively, African Americans have been called "Black Anglo-Saxons" and "Omni-Americans."

Nevertheless, the African American community had to demonstrate, without reservation, its faith in the ideology of America, and its representatives had to demonstrate finesse and astuteness in manipulating the intricate structure of American politics in both the arenas of domestic and foreign policy. In other words, the African American community had to show an inclination to join the establishment. Here among others, Shirley Chisholm, Ralph Bunche, Thurgood Marshall, Andrew Young, Jesse Jackson, Muhammad Ali, Arthur Ashe, and even Bill Cosby with his remarkable Huxtable family of television renown stand as exemplars.

It is reasonable to state, then, that significant steps were made toward the mastering of symbolic politics by the African American community during the 1980s. There was encouragement of the interest of diplomats from African nations in cultivating the African American community. A respected cadre of African American politicians and intellectuals became available to guide and advise in times of international as well as domestic crisis and to caution against what may be termed confrontational or apocalyptic politics. The emergence of Jesse Jackson as a politician of almost impeccable credentials, integrity, and commitment to the support of the essence of American ideals contributed immensely to the cohesion of the African American community and elevated the image of the United States among nations throughout the world.

Nevertheless, with this dynamic thrust of the African American community toward acquiring independent access to the source of power, domination, and control in America — by establishing electoral muscle, developing a lobbying apparatus, and mastering symbolic politics — there was fueled the paradox of creating forces that signaled the possible demise of the African and Jewish American alliance.

THE POLITICS OF ETHNICITY

The above examination of selected national and international forces and developments during the 1980s reveals the apparent shift of the African American community from a strategic posture of confrontation in its civil rights struggle to one of politics; it now ends with a look at an unintended contingency emerging from this strategic adjustment to what can be called a politics of ethnicity. This unintended consequence, moreover, would seem to bear importantly upon the issue of the continuation — and under what conditions — of the African and Jewish American alliance.

Few serious attempts seem to have been made by the African American community to cultivate coalitional relations with the Native American or the Spanish American minority groups. Nevertheless, these

several disparate minority communities of America were not unaware of
the civil rights and the Black Power movements of the African American
community. In fact, it is reasonable to observe that the African American
community, with its heroic civil rights struggle, may have served as a
reference group or model for these particular minority groups. Some
evidence exists of at least exploratory or fugitive contacts between
elements of the African American community with Puerto Rican
nationalists, some Native American nations or tribes, and Chicano or
Mexican American groups.[7]

However, the dominant integration thrust so conspicuous ordinarily
within the civil rights struggle of the African American community
appeared to clash with the basic interests or directions of the Native
American and Spanish American communities. That is, possibly because
of historical and cultural imperatives (and perhaps even a muted "racial"
factor), the essence of the existential reality of Spanish and Native
American groups as minority groups in America produced a uniquely
different ideology vis-à-vis the dominant European American majority
that contrasted significantly with that of the African American
community. This distinctive collective ideology or goal tended to value
independence and freedom higher than such social and cultural
possibilities as assimilation, acculturation, accommodation, and
integration. Illustratively, with respect to schooling, the Chicano or
Mexican American community seemed to prefer autonomous control over
the administration of their public schools rather than, as in the case of the
African American community, so-called integration.

While there is little historical evidence of serious or sustained
coalitional relations between the Chinese, Japanese, and other Asian
American communities and the African American community, there was a
steady arrival during the 1970s and 1980s of competitive new ethnic
immigrants from Asia, the Caribbean, and Central and South America. It
is not unreasonable to suggest the possibility that these new arrivals could
be perceived as potential if not actual threats to the struggles and the
status of both the Jewish and the African American minority
communities.

If defined, however, as potential allies for the African American
community, the mere presence of these other minority communities in the
United States has the possibility of aggravating the now almost constant
estrangement found within the African and Jewish American alliance. It
cannot be overlooked that one of the primary aims of the so-called
Rainbow Coalition of the Jackson presidential campaigns was to attempt
to define clearly a set of political goals for such an African and Spanish

American alliance. Clearly, any such political coalition, if culminated, could only inject additional unresolved contradictions into the historic African and Jewish American alliance.

In brief, the evidence would seem to be conclusive that, during the 1980s, the long-term coalition between the African and Jewish American communities was severely, if not fatally, ruptured. The increased number of bitter clashes characterized by virulent animosity, particularly in large metropolitan areas such as Chicago and New York City, were symptomatic of this estrangement between two minority communities with a laudable historic record of effective coalitional relations. These incidents were newsworthy and were covered in depth, nationally and internationally, by the mass media.[8] Yet, it must be observed that that special relationship traditionally honored between the Jewish and African American communities did not seem to be seriously broached in such metropolitan areas as Philadelphia, Los Angeles, St. Louis, Atlanta, Baltimore, New Orleans, Richmond, Cincinnati, and Miami.

Great care must be taken, then, in attempting to identify the determinants of the apparent collapse of this minority community alliance during this particular period or in prematurely announcing its dissolution. The superficial explanations of anti-Semitism in the African American community and a general mutual intergroup insensitivity to the special interests of each minority community are deemed inadequate for understanding this phase of the coalition process of the alliance. Three critical developments within the changing context of the predicament of minority groups in American society are offered suggestively, therefore, as extending the above explanations of the intransigent estrangement within the African and Jewish American alliance.

First, the Reagan administration, during the 1980s, posed excruciating pragmatic, political, and ideological dilemmas for both the African and the Jewish American communities. A key development during this change from a liberal to a conservative political administration was the broadening in scope of the definition of the concept "minority." The terms of reference, in other words, of the civil rights struggle were radically altered. The implications of this redefinition were of profound significance for the civil rights struggle and especially so for the African American community.

Second, the ideological orientation of the African American community shifted from a direct concern with confrontations over rights, justice, and redress to securing access to the sources of power, domination, and control in American society. Deliberate progress was made by the minority community in renouncing its previous dependent political status and independently attempting to create electoral influence, organize a lobbying capacity, and acquire skill and finesse in the symbolic politics of the nation.

Finally, the heightening of collective consciousness and mobilization of other racial groups (for example, the Native Americans, Spanish Americans, and Asian Americans) into minority communities, as exemplified by the African American community in the civil rights struggle, altered the bargaining positions of both the African and the Jewish American communities. This change complicated immensely that unique special relationship of the African and Jewish American communities. The present rupture in the African and Jewish American alliance, in sum, is best understood as one that has arisen out of a growing redefinition of the African American community as a potential threat to the Jewish American community in influencing the national bases of power, domination, and control.

NOTES

1. An account of this incident and some details of its background are provided by Feuerlicht, *Fates of the Jews*, pp. 175–76, 203–18; and Robert G. Weisbord and Richard Kazarian, Jr., *Israel in the Black American Perspective* (Westport, CT: Greenwood Press, 1985), Chapter 6, "A Confrontation between Friends: The Andrew Young Affair." Also see Kaufman, *Broken Alliance*, p. 246, for some interesting details of the aftermath of the Young resignation.

2. The term *underclass* currently is fashionable or an "in" expression. Its conceptual clarification and rigorous analytical application can be found in the works of Douglas G. Glasgow, *The Black Underclass: Poverty, Unemployment, and Entrapment of Ghetto Youth* (San Francisco: Jossey-Bass, 1980), Chapter 1; and William Julius Wilson, *The Truly Disadvantaged: The Inner City, the Underclass, and Public Policy* (Chicago: University of Chicago Press, 1987). See also Morton M. Kondracke, "The Two Black Americas: Bush's Most Urgent Policy Problem," *The New Republic* (February 6 1989): 17–20.

3. See Frederic E. Wakeman, Jr., "Annual Report of the President, 1987–88," *Social Science Research Council Annual Report* (New York: Social Science Research Council, 1987–88), pp. 13–24.

4. Ibid., p. 14.

5. Derrick Bell, *And We Are Not Saved* (New York: Basic, 1987), pp. 108–17.

6. Charles S. Johnson, *Bitter Canaan: The Story of the Negro Republic* (New Brunswick: Transaction Books, 1987), p. 148.

7. Carson, *In Struggle*, p. 278; and throughout the work of Stan Steiner, *La Raza: The Mexican Americans* (New York: Harper and Row, Inc., 1970).

8. For a most poignant and incisive example of this coverage see Leanita McClain, edited and with an introduction by Clarence Page, *A Foot in Each World: Essays and Articles* (Evanston, IL: Northwestern University Press, 1986).

8

Implications:
Policy and Practice

This effort to disentangle the many subtleties making up the complicated relations that evolved and were sustained over time in American society between two minority groups — the African and Jewish American communities — was grounded in reasons that are both personal and disciplinary. As an African American I was, and remain, obsessed with trying to understand the phenomenon of racism — its origins, manifestations, contributing conditions, metamorphoses, and consequences — in American society.

Practitioners of sociology, from its origin in the nineteenth century in America, have recognized and exploited the saliency of the phenomenon of race for acquiring knowledge about the collective life of man in literally all aspects of the subsequent development of the discipline. It would be difficult, indeed, to overestimate the importance of the play of the concept of race as a factor in the study of human society and for the development of the discipline of sociology.

Curiously, however, that distinct body of phenomena making up the interrelations of minority groups within a racist, pluralistic, democratic society has been comparatively neglected in sociological inquiry. Emphasis has been placed, instead, upon the interrelations between subordinate or minority and dominant or majority groups. Thus, the essential impetus to investigate that particular set of relations, which conventional and scholarly wisdom held connected the African and Jewish minority groups, came from the desires both to satisfy a personal passion and to contribute to mending a possible oversight in scholarly inquiry.

Minority groups are not, nor have they been historically, scarce in American society. The interrelationships of the Jewish and African American minority groups, however, were selected calculatedly for investigation out of the universe of all such sets of minority group relations to be found in American society. It is conceded that all such sets of interactive relations between minority groups may well be worthy of attention from the perspectives of interminority group relations and of public policy making. I believe, however, that historically there was uniqueness of perception, definition, expectation, and experience between the Jewish and African American minority groups that justifies their selection for this particular examination.

I applied a macrosocietal and historical approach because of a primary concern with the developmental character of the relations between these two minority groups and the intrinsic nature of the overwhelming secondary evidence available for examination. Broadly, American society as a whole is the context within which attention was focused upon the relations between the African and Jewish American minorities, and the boundaries or time limits of the examination are from approximately 1890 to 1990.

Because of an overriding concern with the character of the relations (as well as with selected social forces possibly contributing to changes in them) between the African and Jewish American minority groups, a frame of reference was used featuring an emphasis upon collective, or group, interaction and transaction. Notice is taken of that customary tendency in contemporary mainstream sociology to deemphasize the group or collective perspective of much of the race relations inquiry. This predisposition is consonant with the general acceptance of that valuation of the integral position of individualism within the ideology of American culture. In the frame of reference used here, however, a group or collective orientation toward interminority relations is presumed to be more fitting for attempting to understand the appearance and the reality of race in American society.

Negotiation, bargaining, cooperation, and conflict were identified as those processes of interaction to be examined as representing the essence of the relations between the two minority communities. The concerted actions these interactive processes are presumed to represent are conceptualized ultimately as the core of the process of coalition formation or alliance. The attempt was made to interpret the coalitional behavior of the African and Jewish American communities, as historic allies within the race relations configurations of American society, from the general existential perspective of dominance and social power.

The use of the term *community* was of decisive importance in this dissection of the historically intricate relations between the African and Jewish American minority groups. Simply, the term connotes the notion of minority groups having the capacity to act concertedly; because of a unique set of existential experiences, such minority groups tend to identify themselves and be identified by others as a unified collective. Communities, of course, are both identified and solidified as unified collectives by the simultaneous pressures of both external and internal social forces.

Finally, to tease meaning out of the evidence about the relations between the African and Jewish American communities, and about their concerted actions, the following procedures were followed. First, the determination was made that interaction occurred. Second, the attempt was made to ascertain the conditions, reasons for, and expected goals of such collective action. Third, an attempt was made to identify or isolate the means collectively designed to obtain desired goals by concerted actions. The attempt was made, then, to determine the consequences, anticipated and unanticipated, for the African and Jewish American communities of implementing the concerted actions and policies.

I have no doubt that an alliance (some essentially ongoing network of coalitional, combination, partnership, compact-like, arranged, and understood behaviors) existed between the Jewish and African American minority groups in the United States. The evidence examined and analyzed makes this fact conclusive. The deliberate actions of this alliance to interdict the pernicious effects of, or induce change in, major institutional areas and social policies of the nation on behalf of racial justice and of racial equity and equality reveal traits of tenaciousness, ingenuity, and resilience in the face of massive resistance and the sweep of incessant, confounding societal change. The Jewish and African American alliance survived — somehow, and barely — all of this and, hopefully, will persist in surviving, re-creating itself, phoenix-like, to challenge changing needs, situations, and conditions.

Mention must be made of the fact that little formal, public, or official notice ordinarily was made of the existence of this minority group alliance. Its being was not celebrated loudly, probably for strategic reasons. Its renown, reputation, or fame has been nebulous, if not unillustrious, to all but close observers of race relations in the United States.

Meanwhile, however, its potential for contributing to the realms of public policy and the social and policy-making sciences should not be underestimated. For instance, the study of coalitional relations between minority communities in a democratic but racist society may hold profound theoretical implications for the study of the processes of societal transition from authoritarianism now under way in such nations as the Soviet Union, Spain, Portugal, and Italy. Also, the examination of coalition formation and alliances between minority communities may have critical importance as a public policy issue in terms of understanding the role of race as a force for stability or instability in the United States. Close examination of minority community coalitions and alliances could lead to useful knowledge in arenas of controversy about the relative influence of leadership initiative as opposed to elite bargaining in the policy determination process.

I believe, as a result of this attempt to explain what has already occurred, that an urgent need will continue to exist for a "special under-standing" between the Asian, Jewish, Native, Spanish, and African American communities in the United States. Such potential coalitional formations need to commit themselves — in the short as well as long term — to at least two goals: the educational, psychological, political, and economic development of disadvantaged peoples, regardless of race; and the eradication from American society — through close monitoring and severe sanctions — of any preferential treatment for individuals and groups.

THE PASSAGE OF AN ALLIANCE: A SCHEMATIC

Presented below is a diachronically organized, somewhat arbitrary, schematic summary grounded in the above examination of the African and Jewish American alliance.

Phase 1: 1890–1914

Little evidence of negotiation, bargaining, cooperation, or conflict between the two minority groups as collective entities or communities is found during this exploratory or precoalition stage. Essentially the African and Jewish American minority groups were engaged in coping or survival activities, attempting to define what American society really was and to understand what their predicaments were in it. Little conclusive evidence is found during this exploratory phase of a distinct awareness of any overriding mutual interests between the two minority groups; encounters between them were limited apparently to eccentric, individualistic efforts of philanthropy and sporadic individual contacts.

Both minority communities are found to be engaged, largely independently, in developing and elaborating communal organizational structures designed to enhance intragroup solidarity and to represent them responsibly within American society in furthering their own particular survival needs. Many voluntary associations were organized during this watershed time period of American history. Such organizations as the American Jewish Committee, Hadassah, and the American Jewish

Congress were joined by the already existing B'nai B'rith. The National Afro-American League, the National Association of Colored Women, the Niagara Movement, the NAACP, and the National Urban League came into being, largely from needs unique to the African American minority group, during this period.

The slight traces of negotiation and cooperation between the African and Jewish American communities during this exploratory phase of the alliance are to be found in the founding of some of the above, essentially African American, civil rights organizations. Yet the character of such negotiations and cooperations plausibly engaged in during the creation of these vanguard civil rights organizations demonstrates, by all accounts, a distinct lack of parity — or equality of relative status — of the two minority communities in American society.

Phase 2: 1915–1935

The evidence examined indicates conclusively that the initial bonding of the African and Jewish American communities into alliance took place during this second phase of its historic passage. Signs became obvious in American life that indicated grave collective risks for both minority communities. Consequently, definite merging of mutual interests around the constitutional issue of due process (especially with the Supreme Court cases of *Frank* v. *Mangrum* and *Moore* v. *Dempsey*) sealed the felt need to ally the two minority communities, and this resulted, ultimately, in other concrete concerted actions such as, for example, the eventual creation and adoption of the so-called "litigative advocacy" strategy by the alliance.

Philanthropic activities entailing bargaining and negotiation were extensive during this second phase of the alliance. The most visible outcomes of these interactive behaviors, it appears, were some degree of institutionalization of philanthropy from the Jewish American community to the African American community and the emergence from the Jewish American community of that unique expression of communal social responsibility for the African American community labeled the being of-use strategy. These primarily unilaterally determined links of philanthropy and the mutually accepted strategic approaches did much to cement the bonds of the alliance. Furthermore, concern over the problem of lynching violence, culminating in concerted efforts for the ill-fated Dyer Anti-Lynching bill of 1922, elicited considerable cooperation between the two minority communities and served further to legitimate the bonds of the alliance.

The structure of policy determination and decision making within the alliance seems to have been set more firmly into a format of nonparity, and even dependency, of the African American ally during the Harlem Renaissance period of this second phase of the alliance. This essentially avant-garde movement spurred the convergence of artistic and cultural activities into the politics of the arts — the calculated use of creativity and expressiveness as a negotiable power of exchange in the civil rights struggle.

Hegemony in the management of the concerted efforts of the alliance was secured by the Jewish American partner; its assumed official roles within American society of broker, interpreter, intermediary, and champion of and for the African American community were solidified or legitimated. There is a paradox in the fact that the African American partner had come — ostensibly by way of initial differences in community structure, differences in relative societal status, starkly dissimilar historical experiences of oppression, and, possibly, ineexperience in negotiating and bargaining — to occupy a position of subordination, dependency, and inequality within that very instrumentality specifically designed to nullify those precise societal conditions.

The first incipient evidences of conflict between the allies appear during this second phase of the alliance. Symptoms of tensions and strains clearly are observed over the pseudo paternalistic posture of the Jewish American community toward the African American community, and over the evolved hegemonic character of the decision-making and policy-determination structure within the alliance. Other areas of barely suppressed conflict were ideological differences over the stances to be taken toward the programs of the Communist Party and the primacy of the litigative advocacy strategy over an alternative economic and political strategy in resolving the problems of racial injustice and oppression. During this second phase of the alliance, also, there erupted scattered clashes in major urban places, which tended, in general, to be perceived by the Jewish American community as symptoms of an embedded reservoir of anti-Semitism within the African American community, which tended to be perceived by the African American community as symptoms of exploitation and, possibly, as responses to racism.

Phase 3: 1936–1946

The third phase of the alliance is best described as a fairly quiescent stage of coalition formation. This respite from the exigencies of the process of coalitional formation, for both the African and Jewish

American communities, caused by, without doubt, their particular collective needs attendant upon participation in massive societal forces derived largely from situations such as the national and international problems of economic depression, the onset of war in Europe, the atrocity of the Holocaust, a resurgence of the Zionist movement, and the national mobilization for and participation in World War II.

Examples of concerted actions by the alliance are found, however, in the protracted defenses developed out of the internationally famous Scottsboro Boys and Herndon *causes célèbres,* in the implementation of some governmental programs launched to provide relief during the Great Depression, and in some of the attempts launched to overcome the racist ideology as well as the institutionalized racial practices of the military services during World War II.

The African American community continued to be preoccupied, on the ideological level, with that perpetual controversy over the relative efficacy of accommodative versus assimilative strategies in ameliorating its oppressed and pariah status in American society. Doctrinal differences over the tactics of noneconomic liberalism, legal redress, and social and political correctness versus those of political and economic equity continued to provide arenas of tension and strain between the partners of the alliance.

Phase 4: 1946–1958

With the end of World War II and the onset of the legitimation of the United States as a superpower, a period of rapprochement describes best the fourth phase of the African and Jewish American alliance. Close cooperation between the two minority communities is demonstrated by the accord reached by the alliance to pursue to the bitter end the legal attack on racial discrimination and inequality in the public schooling system. This culminated in the U.S. Supreme Court *Brown* decisions of the early 1950s. Similarly, concerted actions by the alliance in the legal arena are undertaken in the social domains of housing, enfranchisement, and employment. These concerted actions are interpreted as the primary catalysts preparatory to the triggering of that pending massive movement toward the nationalization of civil rights throughout American society.

Considerable evidence is found during this fourth phase of the alliance, however, that suggests the emergence of a growing recognition of a possible misalliance between the two minority communities. The Jewish American community had become by this time so absorbed, if not assimilated, into American society as to lose much of the objective meaning of being a minority group, or at least had assumed the attributes of what is termed in race relations theory middleman minority group status. It occupied, legitimately, within American society a structural position of social eminence and power. On the other hand, the generally perceived relative social status of the African American community remained essentially that of a conspicuously deprived, impotent, and pariah minority — exposed generally to those economic conditions described for an exploited group by dual labor market theories — within a democratic society.

Moreover, following the infamy of the Holocaust and the creation of the state of Israel, the attention and interest of the Jewish American community was beginning to be distracted appreciably from the initial and primary civil rights issues that originally faced the alliance. A concrete result of this distraction was what amounted to some erosion of concern for the seemingly intractable problem of racism confronting its principal ally, the African American community. At the same time, the African American community was becoming increasingly skeptical of the promises of the earlier formulated noneconomic liberalism strategy and was moving inexorably toward the development of a serious interest in, and involvement with, the transnational problems attendant upon the independence of African nations following the dismantling of imperialistic colonialism as an aftermath of World War II. Nevertheless, during its fourth phase reconciliation and accord between the allies and with American society at large appear to be the dominant or most prominent feature of the alliance.

Phase 5: 1958–1967

This phase of the alliance — hard upon the immediately preceding fourth phase of rapprochement with its obvious tendency toward nationalization of the civil rights movement — is dominated by attempts to maintain leadership initiative in the nationwide activism for civil rights. The alliance was prominently involved in the implementation of the politics of mass protests accompanied by the escalating response of terror and violence and, as well, with the convoluted strands of mass movements of grievance, unrest, discontent, and nonconformity surfacing throughout the United States. The relations between the allies within the coalition are distinguished from previous coalitional phases by heightened bargaining, negotiation, and cooperation. Almost all aspects of the civil rights movement during this fifth phase of the alliance illustrate the unity and consensus, or solidarity, of the African and Jewish American partners in the struggle toward racial equality and justice.

However, the bankruptcy of the so-called litigative advocacy strategy with respect to the attainment of the substance, rather than the shadow, of the goals of group equity and justice — as shown so clearly at this time by the outcomes of the so-called educational strategy — set off unmistakable indications of a massive discontent within the African American community. In one sense the forces for consensus and unity within the alliance were met with internal as well as external forces contributing to its instability and possible disintegration.

Thus, a rift in the alliance appeared resulting apparently from such issues as factionalism and ideological turmoil among the African American civil rights organizations — largely over the matters of racial separatism and Black Nationalism — and, as well, the matter of organizational hegemony over the African American community. There also began to emerge an intense controversy over the principle of interracialism (in essence, the question of the saliency of race for the issue of group autonomy, control, and power) in the civil rights movement and, as well, the matter of options of other allies on the national as well as international levels. Lively disputes over these issues contributed to the reawakening of a latent sense of divisiveness between the allies within the alliance.

The sense of decreased solidarity within the alliance was compounded, on the other hand, by inexorable pressures exerted on the Jewish American community to make paramount in its concerns the issues of the Holocaust and the survival of the state of Israel. Concern was focused also on what was perceived as disturbing ideological developments and symptoms of alleged anti-Semitism from within the African American community. Predictably, bewilderment, disillusion, and conflict became increasingly prominent qualities of the coalitional relations of the African and Jewish American communities and within the alliance. Nevertheless, what can be conceptualized fairly as the epitome of a model of coalitional behavior between minority communities in pluralistic American society is demonstrated by the calculated and concerted actions of the African and Jewish American allies throughout most of this fifth phase of the alliance.

Phase 6: 1968–1979

Schism, cleavage, and profound disaffection threatened the historic solidarity, if not the actual existence, of the African and Jewish American coalition during this phase of the alliance. Relations between the allies are dominated by myriad forms of conflict. Much of the turbulent interactions of the allies centered ostensibly on the growing legitimation of the so-called Black Power movement, the issue of community control in urban schooling, and implementation of the public policy of affirmative action in the domains of higher education and employment. Regardless of the appearance of extreme differences over these several matters by the allies within the alliance, there was reason to suspect deeper and more fundamental divergence of goal definition, practices, and priorities between the African and Jewish American minority communities.

During this sixth phase of the alliance it became patently clear that the efficacy of some of the fundamental understandings and agreements, which had originally forged and continually supported the coalition between these two minority communities, had been lost. There seemed to be, for example, a lessening of sensitivity to the particular self-interests of each of the partners in the alliance. Much was made, too, of perceived group exploitations rather than mutual benefits stemming from the coalition. Acceptance of the notion that the factor of race itself could be a limiting constraint upon coalition formation was an unusually divisive issue, involving, as it seemed to, implicit questions about group autonomy and dependency, social power, and social control. Finally, considerable dispute arose between the allies over the very nature of the goals of the alliance, provoking intense deliberations over the possible displacement of idealistic and general expectations for concrete and specific coalitional ends. These particular disputes featured, also, bitter recriminations about alignments with other potentially controversial national and international allies.

Phase 7: The 1980s

That special relationship linking the African and Jewish American communities, which endured somehow throughout most of the twentieth century, is fatally ruptured during this phase of the alliance. Despite some slight and intermittent attempts at reconciliation between approximately 1978 and 1982 the predominant character of the relationship during this stage of the alliance can only be described fairly as that of rancorous strife, bitter confrontation, and intense, if not hostile, antagonistic competition. The web of interactions between the African and Jewish American minority communities displays undeniably indications of transformation from the more or less structured processes of a trusted ally into the more or less unstructured ones of a deadly adversary.

The estrangement resulting in this disintegration of the alliance is interpreted as a consequence both of the cumulative effects of latent and long-standing strains and tensions between the coalition partners and, as well, the particularistic adaptations made by both minority communities to social changes imminent in American society. The acerbity surrounding the apparent disintegration of the alliance, it is argued, cannot be understood by such superficial explanations as endemic anti-Semitism in the African American community; mutual intergroup insensitivities to the special self-interests of each of the partners; the asymmetrical, unbalanced structure of authority and influence within the coalition; the stance of patronizing arrogance toward the African American community allegedly held by the Jewish American community; and the barrage of vociferous objections raised about foreign policy positions taken by the African American community.

Interpretation of the available evidence suggests, rather, that the increasing divisiveness within the alliance at this time is more reasonably understood as, on one hand, a consequence of an altered collective consciousness or self-identity of, and a massively ingrained sense of discontent and grievance within, the African American community. From these existential realities ensued a fundamental process of reassessment, objectively and subjectively, of its role or fate as a racial minority in pluralistic American society. This reassessment, it is held, resulted in a basic reorientation of the African American community of its strategic role in American society. This strategic reorientation of the African American community is countered by an essentially implacable response of resentment and antagonism from the Jewish American community whose paramount concerns had crystallized into the intertwined issues of the universal fate of that distinct sense of Jewish consciousness and the survival of the state of Israel.

The strategic ideological reorientation of the African American community would seem to be best understood as a marked shift of emphasis from the immediate and direct confrontation with the symptomatic problems or conditions of civil rights oppression, inequality, and injustice to a calculated pragmatic emphasis upon the more substantive issues of attaining access to and cultivating influence in the political structures and processes of dominance, social power, and social control in American society. This interpretation of this redefinition of the African American community and the redirection of its collective efforts is reached on the basis of the apparent convergence of several key developments during the decade within American society.

The key development first was the transition from a liberal to a conservative ideology throughout American society. This insidious ideological transformation was an especially prominent feature of the federal government during the Republican administration of President Ronald Reagan. An immediate consequence of the suzerainty of this conservative ideology was, at least, the conspicuous diminution of concern about the resistant implacability of racism in the nation. This reduction of concern could be interpreted, as well, as the deliberate attempts to counteract or nullify recently acquired gains toward the legitimation of democratic pluralism involving progress, throughout the nation, toward the achievement of racial equality and justice. Calculated attempts were made, openly, to reverse national and local social policy initiatives that would provide relief for the problems inherent in an ethnic and racially diverse society. The cruelty was compounded by the inclusion of antipoverty measures in these efforts, too.

The second key development was a subtle but objective redirection — collective reidentification — of the African American community toward the deliberate and independent pursuit of social power in American society. A consequence, in large part, of this metamorphosis was the emergence of a perception within the Jewish American community of the potential threat posed by the African American community within the open political system of American society.

Finally, the heightening of collective consciousness and the subsequent movements toward mobilization of other aggrieved minority groups was an unexpected development that infinitely complicated the historical struggle of the alliance for human and civil rights in American society. Other minority communities, for example, Native Americans, Spanish Americans, and Asian Americans, now became available as potential allies for coalition into long- as well as short-term alliances.

ILLATION AND PROGNOSIS

It cannot be denied that after centuries of slavery and then decades of heroic and unremitting struggle against almost unyielding racial repression and exploitation the ideals and principles of American democracy still do not apply in practice as equitably to those who comprise the African American community as they do to other, and especially European American, citizens. Neither can it be denied that significant changes have occurred among those social and cultural realities in American society that contribute to the determination and maintenance of the relative status of the African American community. In spite of this knowledge, it would be perilous for social planners and policy makers to deny, in terms of the future, that the United States is becoming an increasingly multiracial society. It is well known, also, that change in public policies with implications for racism is hardly apt to be solely the result of the direct application of sociological prognosis. Nevertheless, the preceding examination of the conduct of a coalition between two minority communities, dedicated to engagement in a struggle to attain the basic principles of American democracy, reveals a historic passage over time that is at once a triumph and a tragedy of the human condition.

The tragic dimensions of the historic passage of the African and Jewish American alliance are marked in the disparate existential realities of the two minority communities within American society. Both minority communities can only acknowledge that their coalition or alliance has not fully accomplished its fundamental purpose of assuring for themselves, and for all Americans, the promises of equality and social justice held out by the tenets of American democracy. A condition of resentment chronically permeates the African American community over its perceived and its objective status in the nation and over the profound and unrelieved resistance met in all attempts — whether collective or individual — to alter this situation. Fear, suspicion, and anxiety are endemic throughout the Jewish American community, notwithstanding its near absorption, if not assimilation, into the mainstream of American society.

For the nation, the continued significance of racism and anti-Semitism — in their myriad manifestations of inequality, social injustice, and rejection — throughout almost all aspects of American society continues to exact exorbitant costs of every conceivable aspect of the human condition. It is conceivable, for example, that the constitutional right to free speech could be seriously threatened by those actions of the lobby of the Jewish American community that allegedly are designed, out of the communal background of fear and anxiety, to suppress opposition and stifle dissent. Findley observes:

> The [Jewish American] lobby has already attained strength far beyond the level its numbers would suggest. Those active in its ranks constitute a tiny part of the population of the United States, but their demographic concentration in states critical to deciding national elections, combined with their unique ability to mobilize campaign resources and public opinion, gives them influence in the political process far out of proportion to their numbers. Even more significant is the remarkable commitment and devotion which lobby partisans bring to their cause. They give generously of their time,

money and energy. Many are leaders in government, public information, education and politics. Their activities are supported by the government of Israel, openly through its embassy in Washington and consulates in our major cities and clandestinely through the extensive operations that Mossad, Israel's foreign intelligence service, undertakes throughout the United States.[1]

The tragedy revealed in the historical passage of the African and Jewish American alliance, in essence, is that there still remains a need in America for its existence. Telling the truth about the troubles of race and anti-Semitism, at all times, is and will most likely continue to be an imperative for the sustenance of the ideal of pluralistic democracy in American society.

The saga of its existence, as well as the mystery of its origination, constitute the triumph found in the historical passage of the African and Jewish American alliance. That two minority communities entangled within the contradictions of the expectations and promises of a value system stubbornly at odds with existential reality could discover or identify each other; reconnoiter their common interests within an intrinsically hostile social context; create a combination to further these mutual concerns against intransigence; and, in fact, exert some influence upon the basic institutions of the nation for almost a century merits celebration.

The odyssey of the African and Jewish American alliance, in its quest for the grail of full acceptance and inclusion in American democracy, provides a glimpse of a type of relationship between two minority groups with "stranger" or "outsider" definitions in a racially organized, intrinsically hostile society. One is made curious about the outcome of the alliance if, hypothetically, other racial minority groups had been included in the coalition or if other sets of minority groups had become consistent allies. One significant residual of the triumph of the alliance, notwithstanding the present appearance of general disarray or misalliance, is the certainty that in some urban areas of the nation — for example, Los Angeles — it continues to wield potent political and civic influence.

It seems, too, that this examination of the relations between two minority groups within a pluralistic society provides eloquent testimony for possible contributions to be made toward fuller understanding of the dynamics of race relations by specific analysis of the interrelationships of minority groups. Moreover, this examination demonstrates the serious need, in that search for usable social science knowledge in race relations, for concrete analyses of intraminority group relations, for example, between the several subcategories of the African Diaspora represented in the African American community and the several subcategories of the Jewish Diaspora represented in the Jewish American community. The revealed play, within minority group relations, of the forces of social power, social control, and the sweep of social change provides subversive evidence about the reality of racism and the continued need for minority group alliances within the pluralistic and open political system of American society.

My final point concerns the designation of the African and Jewish American alliance as unillustrious. What this means is that this coalition of two minority groups, in almost a century of heroic struggle, did not achieve its supreme objective of eliminating that profound gap between the practice and the profession of the ideals of democracy in American society. By no means, however, do I believe that the existence of coalition between the African and Jewish American communities has been futile or that it should be discontinued. The future of American society, it would seem, will increasingly depend upon the potentially invaluable contributions of coalitions of minority groups — without the stigmatizing formation of racially driven hierarchy — to the determination of public policy.

National public policy is not static. I believe that in the effort to achieve equality and social justice for racial minority groups in America the primary initiative, aside from that of the efforts of the minority groups themselves, must rest upon the federal government. Major changes in public policy clearly seem to correspond closely with periods of national trauma and upheaval, and minority group coalitions and alliances can be illustrious in exploiting if not inducing such conditions of social change. In this way will American life be enriched and, possibly, knowledge be acquired.

NOTE

1. Paul Findley, *They Dared to Speak Out: People and Institutions Confront Israel's Lobby* (Westport, CT: Lawrence Hill, 1985), p. 316.

Appendix:
Selected Organizations of the Civil Rights Struggle

1775	The Pennsylvania Society for Promoting the Abolition of Slavery, The Relief of Free Negroes Unlawfully Held in Bondage, and for Improving the Condition of the African Race.
1776	Masonic Order, African Lodge #1; Prince Hall affiliation. Boston, MA.
1787	The Free African Society founded by Richard Allen and Absalom Jones. Philadelphia, PA.
1788	Founding of the first church in the United States by Africans or descendants of Africans, the First African Baptist Church, Savannah, GA.
1794	Founding of Mother Bethel African Methodist Episcopal Church and St. Thomas African Episcopal Church by Richard Allen and Absalom Jones, respectively, in Philadelphia, PA.
1833	American Anti-Slavery Society, Philadelphia, PA.
1840	American and Foreign Anti-Slavery Society, NY.
1843	B'nai B'rith (Sons of the Covenant).
1856	Establishment of the first African American college, Wilberforce University. Wilberforce, OH.
1869	Knights of Labor, Philadelphia, PA. Uriah S. Stephens. International Workingmen's Association, NY. Friedrich A. Sorge. Colored National Labor Union, Washington, DC.
1886	Colored National Farmers Alliance and Cooperative Union, Houston, TX.
1887–1908	National Afro-American League.
1896	National Association of Colored Women. Mary Church Terrell and Mary McLeod Bethune.

1900	Pan African Conference (London). W. E. B. Du Bois.
1905	The Niagara Movement. W. E. B. Du Bois.
1906	American Jewish Committee. Louis Marshall.
1909	The National Association for the Advancement of Colored People (NAACP).
1910	The National Urban League.
1913	American Jewish Congress. Rabbi Stephen Wise.
1914/1925	The Universal Negro Improvement and Conservation Association (UNIA) and African Communities League. Marcus M. Garvey.
Early 1920s	Ethiopian Hebrew Synagogue, NY. Rabbi Wentworth Matthew.
1921	The Workers (Communist) Party, Chicago, IL and NY. Charles E. Ruthenburg.
1922	Anti-Defamation League of B'nai B'rith.
1925	American Negro Labor Congress. Chicago, IL. James W. Ford.
1929	United League of United Latin American Citizens (LULAC), TX.
1931	The Lost-Found Nation of Islam in the Wilderness of North America (also known as The Nation of Islam and as The Black Muslims), Detroit, MI. Elijah Muhammad.
1942	Congress of Racial Equality (CORE), Chicago, IL.
1948	Community Service Organization (CSO), Los Angeles, CA. Eduardo Roybal, Anthony Rios, Fred Ross.
1957	Southern Christian Coordinating Conference (SCLC), Atlanta, GA. Martin Luther King, Jr.
1960	Student Nonviolent Coordinating Committee (SNCC), Raleigh, NC. John Lewis, Robert Moses, and James Forman.
1965	Deacons for Defense and Justice, LA. Black Panther Party (earlier called the Lowndes County Freedom Organization), AL.
1966	Latin American Defense Organization, Chicago, IL. Obed Lopez.
1966/1969	La Crusada Para la Justicia (The Crusade for Justice), Denver, CO. Rodolfo "Corky" Gonzales.
1967	Black Panther Party for Self-Defense, CA.

SOURCES

Lenora E. Berson, *The Negroes and the Jews* (New York: Random House, 1971), pp. 96–111.

Clayborne Carson, *In Struggle: SNCC and The Black Awakening of the 1960s* (Cambridge: Harvard University Press, 1981).

Kenneth Clark, "The Civil Rights Movement," *Daedalus* 95:1 (Winter 1966): 241–64.

Harold Cruse, *Plural but Equal* (New York: William Morrow, 1987), especially pp. 1–24.

William Z. Foster, *The Negro People in American History* (New York: International Publishers, 1954), Chapters 32, 34, 35, and 42.

C. Eric Lincoln, *The Black Muslims in America* (Boston: Beacon Press, 1961).

August Meier and Elliott Rudwick, *CORE: A Study in the Civil Rights Movement, 1942–1968* (Urbana: University of Illinois Press, 1975).

Eileen Southern, *The Music of Black Americans: A History* (New York: W. W. Norton, 1983).

Stan Steiner, *La Raza: The Mexican Americans* (New York: Harper & Row, 1970).

Bibliographic Essay

While a graduate student at the University of Chicago during the 1950s I met Oliver Cromwell Cox at a small dinner party. He was engaged in unsupported research at the university while on a leave from his professorial duties in what some may call the academic hinterlands of America. That evening was tremendously exciting and inspiring for me, primarily because of his iconoclastic skepticism and incisiveness about many subtle aspects of race relations in the United States. His playful yet profound seriousness about race relations scholarship became etched indelibly in my memory.

Cox died in 1974. On learning of this I decided to spend a few hours in the Rutgers University library reading some of his more recent publications. My initial interest in the interrelationships between minority groups in American society can be dated from those few hours spent with the works, and my memories, of Cox. For there I encountered his article entitled "Jewish Self-Interest in 'Black Pluralism'" in *The Sociological Quarterly* 15 (Spring 1974): 183–98. In reflective mulling over this article I came to the decision that the interrelation of minority groups in America was a topic deserving serious scholarly study.

Heretofore, as it is now recalled, I apparently had been oblivious of that emphasis placed by mainstream race relations scholarship largely upon the interrelationships of minority groups with the dominant or superordinate group and to what amounts to an exclusion of concern about the relations between minority groups. This is not the place to attempt to explore why this curious tilting occurs, although, in my judgment, such an exploration into a possible foible of the epistemology of mainstream sociology is pertinent to gaining knowledge about race relations in American society. It became my purpose, then, following the insight gained from Cox, to examine with some care that scholarship purporting to be concerned with the relations between two particular

minority groups (the African and Jewish American communities) perceived as subordinate entities within the context of essentially dominant
European American, Anglo-Saxon Protestant society.

There is no lack of comprehensive bibliographies in the study of race
relations and in both African and Jewish American studies. The works
selected to be mentioned here — classified under the headings of
books, journals, and other sources — are those that were used directly
and are considered indispensable for the arguments that are advanced in
the text.

My interpretations of the origin, evolution, and consequences of the
relations between the African and Jewish American communities vary
some from many of the works to be cited. I am persuaded, for instance,
that an alliance existed. In this conclusion I am supported by the works of
David Lewis, Hasia Diner, Eli Evans, Jonathan Kaufman, and Arthur
Hertzberg. Adolph Reed, Jr., accepts the reality of an alliance but insists
that it was operative through elite-driven formal advocacy organizations.
Roberta Feuerlicht concludes that, while an alliance existed, it was
regionally grounded and segmental. Harold Cruse and Robert Weisbord
and Arthur Stein are more cautious. They acknowledge, and document,
the apparent existence of a unique affinity or linkage between the African
and Jewish American communities but hesitate to label it a coalition or
alliance. Oliver C. Cox and Alphonso Pinkney argue, on the other hand,
that because of immutable antagonisms and unequal relative social status
between these two minority groups there is little basis for conceiving of
their relationship as an alliance.

BOOKS

The experiences of the Jewish American community have been the
subject of many books. The following were most instructive for me:
Lenore E. Berson, *The Negroes and the Jews* (New York: Random
House, 1971); Hasia R. Diner, *In the Almost Promised Land* (Westport,
CT: Greenwood, 1977); Daniel J. Elazar, *Community and Polity: The
Organizational Dynamics of American Jewry* (Philadelphia: The Jewish
Publication Society of America, 1976); Eli N. Evans, *The Provincials: A
Personal History of Jews in the South* (New York: Times, 1983);
Roberta S. Feuerlicht, *The Fates of the Jews* (New York: Times, 1983);
Paul Findley, *They Dared to Speak Out: People and Institutions Confront
Israel's Lobby* (Westport, CT: Lawrence Hill, 1985); Arthur Hertzberg,
The Jews in America: Four Centuries of an Uneasy Encounter: A History
(New York: Simon & Schuster, 1989); especially Paul Johnson, *A

History of the Jews (New York: Harper & Row, 1987); Jonathan Kaufman, *Broken Alliance* (New York: Scribner's Sons, 1988); Abraham D. Lavender, ed., *A Coat of Many Colors* (Westport, CT: Greenwood, 1977); Marcia Graham Synnott, *The Half-Opened Door: Discrimination and Admissions at Harvard, Yale, and Princeton, 1900– 1970* (Westport, CT: Greenwood, 1979); Robert G. Weisbord & Arthur Stein, *Bittersweet Encounters* (Westport, CT: Negro Universities Press, 1970); and Louis Wirth, *The Ghetto* (Chicago: University of Chicago, 1956).

Historical context and selected forces of social change are given prominence in my examination of the coalition formation or the alliance of the African and Jewish American communities. My accounts of the general background for the several decades or periods within which the interplay between the African and Jewish American communities unfolds are indebted heavily to the following: Frederick Lewis Allen, *Only Yesterday* (New York: Perennial, 1931); E. Digby Baltzell, *The Protestant Establishment* (New York: Vintage, 1964); William Z. Foster, *The Negro People in American History* (New York: International, 1970); Raul Hilberg, *The Destruction of the European Jews* (Chicago: Quadrangle, 1961); Paul Johnson, *A History of the Modern World* (London: Weidenfeld & Nicolson, 1983); Hans J. Morgenthau, *The Purpose of American Politics* (New York: Knopf, 1960); Gustavus Myers, *History of Bigotry in the U.S.* (New York: Capricorn, 1960); Cabell Phillips, *The 1940s* (New York: Macmillan, 1975); Arthur M. Schlesinger, Jr., *The Cycles of American History* (Boston: Houghton Mifflin, 1985); Trent Schroyer, *The Critique of Domination* (Boston: Beacon, 1973); and Page Smith, *Redeeming the Time* (New York: McGraw-Hill, 1987).

The histories of the African American community and of the struggle for civil rights in America have received much attention. Indispensable sources for examining these subjects and the alliance of the African and Jewish American communities are: Houston A. Baker, Jr., *Blues, Ideology and Afro-American Literature* (Chicago: University of Chicago Press, 1984); James Baldwin, ed., *Black Anti-Semitism and Jewish Racism* (New York: Baron, 1969); Derick Bell, *And We Are Not Saved: The Elusive Quest for Racial Justice* (New York: Basic, 1979); James E. Blackwell, *The Black Community: Diversity and Unity* (New York: Harper & Row, 1975); Rhoda L. Blumberg, *Civil Rights: The 1960s Freedom Struggle* (Boston: Hall, 1984); Pierre Bourdieu & Jean-Claude Passeron, *Reproduction: In Education, Society and Culture* (London: Sage, 1977); Samuel Bowles & Herbert Gintis, *Schooling in Capitalist*

America (New York: Basic, 1976); Henry Allen Bullock, *A History of Negro Education in the South* (New York: Praeger, 1970); Stokely Carmichael & Charles V. Hamilton, *Black Power: The Politics of Liberation in America* (New York: Vintage, 1967); Clayborne Carson, *In Struggle: SNCC and the Black Awakening of the 1960s* (Cambridge: Harvard, 1981); Oliver C. Cox, *Caste, Class & Race* (New York: Doubleday, 1948); Edmund D. Cronon, *Black Moses: The Story of Marcus Garvey and the Universal Negro Improvement Association* (Madison: University of Wisconsin Press, 1969); especially Harold Cruse, *The Crisis of the Negro Intellectual* (New York: Columbia University Press, 1967); and Harold Cruse, *Plural but Equal* (New York: Morrow, 1987); David J. Garrow, *Bearing the Cross* (New York: Morrow, 1986); James A. Geschwender, ed., *The Black Revolt* (Englewood Cliffs, NJ: Prentice-Hall, 1971); Paula Giddings, *When and Where I Enter: The Impact of Black Women on Race and Sex in America* (New York: Morrow, 1984); Raymond L. Hall, ed., *Black Separatism and Social Reality* (New York: Pergamon, 1977); Louis R. Harlan, *Booker T. Washington,* 2 volumes (New York: Oxford, 1972, 1983); especially David L. Lewis, *When Harlem Was in Vogue* (New York: Knopf, 1981); Manning Marable, *Black American Politics* (London: Verso, 1985); Doug McAdams, *Political Process and the Development of Black Insurgency, 1930–1970* (Chicago: University of Chicago Press, 1982); Albert Murray, *The Omni-Americans* (New York: Outerbridge & Dienstfrey, 1970); Mark Naison, *Communists in Harlem During the Depression* (Urbana: University of Illinois, 1983); Bernard C. Nalty, *Strength for the Fight: A History of Black Americans in the Military* (New York: Free Press, 1986); William M. Phillips, Jr., *The School Sociologist: A Need and an Emergent Profession* (Washington, DC: University Press of America, 1981); Alphonso Pinkney, *The Myth of Black Progress* (Cambridge: Oxford, 1984); Adolph L. Reed, Jr., *The Jesse Jackson Phenomenon* (New Haven, CT: Yale, 1986); Leslie Catherine Sanders, *The Development of Black Theater in America: From Shadows to Selves* (Baton Rouge: Louisiana State University, 1988); Eileen Southern, *The Music of Black Americans* (New York: Norton, 1983); Robert Weisbord, *Freedom Bound* (New York: Norton, 1990); Robert G. Weisbord & Richard Kazarian, Jr., *Israel in the Black American Perspective* (Westport, CT: Greenwood, 1985); Harvie J. Wilkerson III, *From Brown to Bakke* (New York: Oxford, 1979); and Robin M. Williams, *Mutual Accommodation* (Minneapolis: University of Minnesota, 1977).

JOURNALS

Some of the most authoritative work on the African and Jewish American alliance is to be found in the periodical literature. The following articles and essays were most useful: Edna Bonacich, "A Theory of Middleman Minorities," *American Sociological Review* 38 (October 1973): 583–94; Robert Chrisman, "The Crisis of Harold Cruse," *The Black Scholar* 1 (November 1969): 76; Lucy Davidowicz, "The Holocaust Was Unique in Intent, Scope, and Effect," *The Center Magazine* 14 (July/August 1981): 56–64; Vincent Harding, "The Black Wedge in America: Struggle, Crisis and Hope," *The Black Scholar* 7 (December 1975): 28–30, 35–46; Richard D. Hecht, "The Face of Modern Anti-Semitism," *The Center Magazine* 14 (March/April 1981): 17–36; Nathan I. Huggins, "Afro-Americans: National Character and Community," *The Center Magazine* 7 (July/August 1974): 51–66; Betsy Levin & Willis D. Hawley, eds., "School Desegregation: Lessons on the First Twenty-Five Years," *Law and Contemporary Problems* 42 (Summer/Autumn, 1978); especially David L. Lewis, "Parallels and Divergences: Assimilationist Strategies of Afro-American and Jewish Elites from 1910 to the Early 1930s," *The Journal of American History* 71 (December 1984): 543–64; Harvey Molotch, "American Jews and the State of Israel," *The Center Magazine* 16 (May/June 1983): 8–26; Karl-Dieter Opp, "Grievances and Participation in Social Movements," *American Sociological Review* 53 (December 1988): 853–64; W. M. Phillips, Jr., "Race Relations In Cuba: Some Reflections," *The Review of Black Political Economy* 8 (Winter 1978): 173–83; Alphonso Pinkney, "Recent Unrest Between Blacks and Jews: The Claims of Anti-Semitism and Reverse Discrimination," *The Black Sociologist* 8 (Fall-Summer 1978/79): 38–57; Bernard J. Siegel, "Defensive Structuring and Environmental Stress," *American Journal of Sociology* 76 (July 1970): 11–21; Kenneth S. Tollett, "What Led to Bakke," *The Center Magazine* 11 (January/February 1978): 2; and Milton J. Yinger, "Countercultures and Social Change," *American Sociological Review* 42 (December 1977): 849.

OTHER SOURCES

While preparing this book the following works were of special value in supplementing the previously mentioned materials of this bibliographic essay: Kenneth B. Clark, "The Civil Rights Movement: Momentum and

Organization" in *The Black Revolt,* ed. James A. Geschwender (Englewood Cliffs, NJ: Prentice-Hall, 1971), p. 47; especially Harold Cruse, "My Jewish Problem and Theirs," in *Black Anti-Semitism and Jewish Reaction,* ed. James Baldwin (New York: Baron, 1969), pp. 144–88; especially Lucy Davidowicz, "A Century of Jewish History, 1881–1981: The View from America," in *Jewish American Yearbook,* by the American Jewish Committee (New York: The Jewish Publication Society of America, 1981), pp. 97–98; Raymond S. Franklin, "The Political Economy of Black Power," in *The Black Revolt,* ed. James A. Geschwender (Englewood Cliffs, NJ: Prentice-Hall, 1971), pp. 224–30; William A. Gamson, "A Theory of Coalition Formation," in *Small Groups: Studies in Social Interaction,* ed. A. Paul Hare (New York: Knopf, 1965), pp. 562–77; especially C. Eric Lincoln, foreword to *Bittersweet Encounter,* by Robert G. Weisbord & Arthur Stein (Westport, CT: Negro Universities Press, 1970); especially Bayard Rustin, "The Civil Rights Struggle" and "The Failure of Black Separatism," in *A Symposium: Negro-Jewish Relations in the United States,* by the Conference on Jewish Social Studies (New York: Citadel, 1966); especially Edward W. Said, "An Ideology of Difference," in *Writing and Difference,* ed. Henry Louis Gates, Jr. (Chicago: University of Chicago Press, 1986), p. 38; and August Wilson, "Preface to 'Fences,'" in *Playbill* 87 (April 1987): 26.

Index

About the Author

William M. Phillips, Jr., is professor emeritus, Rutgers University. Trained as a sociologist, Phillips taught at the Arkansas A., M. & N. College (now the University of Arkansas at Pine Bluff) and Rutgers, and is the author of *The School Sociologist,* co-author of *Trouble in Our Community,* and author of numerous articles.